Archaeo-Volunteers

The World Guide to Archaeological and Heritage Volunteering

Green Volunteers
Publications

Archaeo-Volunteers
The World Guide to Archaeological and Heritage Volunteering

Editors:	Fabio Ausenda and Erin McCloskey, assisted by Francesco Foresti and Arianna Luna Lasorsa
Cover design:	Studio Cappellato e Laurent srl, Roberta Romagnoni, Milano
Cover photo:	Volunteers at work at 'Thanet Earth' (Kent, UK) Bronze Age site of the Canterbury Archaeological Trust.
Acknowledgements:	Special thanks to the Canterbury Archaeological Trust www.canterburytrust.co.uk

This Guide is not an annual publication: the useful websites section, the online Project Database on www.archaeovolunteers.org and the link page of our website (see bottom of next page) allow the reader to find continuous new opportunities and to keep the information in this Guide always up to date.

Published by:	Green Volunteers di Fabio Ausenda Via Canonica 72 - 20154 Milano, Italy www.greenvolunteers.com e-mail: green@greenvolunteers.org

US & Canada distribution:	Universe Publishing A division of Rizzoli International Publications, Inc. 300 Park Avenue South, New York, NY 10010
UK distribution:	Crimson Publishing A division of Crimson Business Westminster House, Kew Road, Richmond TW9 2ND, England
Australia and New Zealand distribution:	Woodslane Pty Ltd Unit 7/5 Vuko Place Warriewood NSW 2102
Printed in Jan. 2009 by:	Consorzio Artigiano L.V.G. srl, Azzate (VA), Italy

ISBN: 978-88-89060-15-5
Library of Congress Control Number: 2008943206

The Editors highly recommend the following introductory pages are read. These pages explain what humanitarian and development volunteering involves and will increase the volunteer's chances of being accepted by an organisation.

HOW TO FIND MANY MORE ORGANISATIONS TO VOLUNTEER FOR AND HOW TO KEEP THIS GUIDE UPDATED:

The "useful websites" section (see page 21) and the Online Database on our website www.archaeovolunteers.org, constantly updated with new projects, allow the reader to find hundreds of other organisations in the UK, US, Canada, Australia, Europe, and in other countries offering various volunteering opportunities worldwide. Our Online Database is frequently updated, allowing the reader to constantly find new opportunities. Please see www.archeovolunteers.org how to join the Archaeovolunteers Database. A simple proof of ownership of the book will be asked.

TABLE OF CONTENTS

INTRODUCTION

Although the title is *Archaeo-Volunteers*, the scope of the Guide include organisations and projects involved in archaeology, anthropology, cultural heritage and awareness, historical restoration and maintenance, and palaeontology. Archaeology, and its related fields, provide a fascinating and lifelong pastime for anyone with an interest and is not an exclusively professional arena. Amateurs and enthusiasts have important roles to play and can do valuable work. Most projects are led by experienced archaeologists, palaeontologists, or other scientists and specialists to teach volunteers and students new skills and information. The following definitions provide a general description and overview of the major fields of discipline and the sectors occupied by this guide.

Archaeology is a subfield of anthropology. It is the study of the material remains and environmental effects of past human activities. These investigations can be of the recent past to millions of years ago. The study involves that of cultural processes through looking at the remains of past human behaviour including old farm field systems and housing. They can reveal insights about the migrations of human habitation, to the early adoption of agriculture, to the development of industries, to the origin and possible demise of ancient civilisations, etc., through the discovery of entire lost cities down to the discovery of microscopic remains of flora or fauna associated with human activities. Archaeology forms interdisciplinary approaches to research by collaborating with many other disciplines, including geography, history, social sciences, maths, physics, biology, chemistry, art, religion, and technology.

Anthropology can be considered a four-field discipline that studies human culture. Archaeology, as defined above, is one of these subfields. However, beyond archaeology is physical/biological anthropology, which focuses on primates and human biology; social/cultural anthropology, which studies present or the recent past human societies; and linguistic or socio-linguistic anthropology, which is the study of human language. It could be argued that medical anthropology and applied anthropology are two additional an emerging subfields.

Palaeontology is the branch of archaeology that studies fossil organisms and related remains of life of past geological ages. It is the study of plant and animal lifeforms that provide evolutionary clues to understand the relationship between present species and their ancient ancestors, how their development led to their present forms, and which factors, such as behaviour and environment, were catalysts to their evolution and survival or, contrarily, their extinction.

Cultural Heritage and Historical Restoration is not a defined science but a categorisation established for the purpose of defining this sector with the Guide. The recognition of sites of cultural significance such as buildings, structures, or gardens allow for the preservation of heritage to be appreciated by visitors as well as the local community and its future generations. These areas are often within or of themselves World Heritage sites as they have been defined by UNESCO - United Nations Educational, Scientific and Cultural Organisation, or government protected historical sites.

ARCHAEOLOGICAL FIELDWORK

Archaeology is a fascinating and even romantic field of discovery for a traveller. However, do not be disillusioned by its Hollywood glamour; it is hard work! Do not expect to be unearthing vast chambers of forgotten treasures. Your entire dig experience may be within a single square meter of substrate that you excavate with a tiny pick and a brush. It may involve only uncovering small broken fragments of pottery or the remains of a small wall. There is always the possibility though of discovering the unexpected, and the tangible connection to history by discovering an artefact that is thousands of years old is a privileged and thrilling experience. Ultimately, you are given the opportunity to contribute personally to the recovery and preservation of the past.

Excavation opportunities tend to fall under one of three categories: training courses, amateur digs, or day digs. The training courses are offered through universities and colleges with well-established archaeology, palaeontology, or anthropology departments. The field school is typically one or two weeks or more in the summer doing field survey or excavation with PhD students conducting research. These projects may not be open to non-students if competition for positions is high. Amateur digs are conducted by a research institution independently or in conjunction with an expedition company. The Earthwatch Institute is an example of an organisation where the volunteer requires no skills or experience and works alongside professional scientists in the field. This organisation is very reputable and the experience is bound to be rewarding but the cost to join is on the high end of the scale. Smaller projects offer similar programmes but undoubtedly have fewer resources and volunteers may have a 'rougher' experience. However, every project differs in accommodation and style; even with Earthwatch you may find yourself in a remote area, sleeping in a tent, and eating limited cuisine. Volunteering with a smaller organisation is more economically affordable and may be more rewarding in the sense that your volunteer contribution may be the lifeblood of the project's revenue. Without volunteer support in developing countries, valuable research would possibly not occur. However, always research the organisation well before joining and ensure that the programme is professional, trustworthy, and safe. Projects that are organised in conjunction with an expedition company will have several tourist and educative excursions built into the programme in order for the volunteers to discover the local area and culture. The third type of excavation category is the day dig. This type of programme is open to the public and often all ages are accommodated. Day digs are typically set at a museum site with staff supervision and instruction and are aimed at tourists, with individual, family, or school rates to participate in the programme. Alternatively the excavation may be organised through a small community organisation where local enthusiasts volunteer on a weekend or evening basis. These digs are free but offer no accommodation, meals, or transportation, and the volunteers may have to join the society in order to be covered by the project's insurance.

Archaeological excavation is often labour intensive and prospective volunteers should understand their physical ability and stamina before joining. Excavation is often considered the most exciting aspect of the work, but it is also the most physically demanding. Hours are spent kneeling or stooping, lifting and carrying, or digging with picks and shovels. Excavated soil is carried in buckets or bags to a sorting area that may be in close proximity to the dig or a fair distance walk off site. Work may be performed in heat or rain, in cold wind, or at high elevations. Higher elevations may make physical work seem more strenuous. Remote sites and survey work involves hiking, possibly up and down steep inclines or across difficult terrain. Fully understand what physical work is expected from the volunteers and whether you are able to meet this demand. Notify the project in advance of health concerns such as asthma or allergies. Reconstruction and excavation sites can be very dusty or in grassy fields.

Health and safety is the concern of the volunteer as well as the project or organisation. Even if insurance is provided it is always wise to have your own personal coverage against accident or illness, trip cancellation or early return, etc. Anti-tetanus vaccination is recommended and may be mandatory on some sites. Hygiene conditions are often very basic in the field. Organics or groundwater seepage in the soil dictates washing your hands after digging and before eating. It has been suggested that cattle bones found in the soil can still carry viable germs such as anthrax, hoof and mouth disease, etc., although this has never been proven. If the field setting offers no clean water with which to wash, dry soap or disinfectant may be a good idea to carry along with you. Archaeological fieldwork has risks owing to the physical demands and the work setting. Deep stratification, unstable masonry, shoring and scaffolding, unstable deposits, and groundwater seepage all pose hazards. The project should supply safety equipment and take all precautions to ensure a safe worksite. However, use your own common sense and best judgement and do not put yourself in an uncomfortable or dangerous situation.

Beyond Excavation

There is more to archaeology than excavation. There is considerable work that is undertaken in the laboratory processing and archiving finds. Volunteers can also become involved in setting up museum displays and public outreach programmes. Cultural programmes that focus more on anthropological study of culture involves participants more in community projects, festivals, and cultural exchanges, and there are also the historical restoration projects where volunteers help restore architecture or other significant structures requiring preservation. Some cultural programmes referenced in this guide tour cities and villages and museums offering an educational tour rather than a work situation.

WHY VOLUNTEER?

The philosophy behind voluntary work as an alternative vacation is one of reciprocal favour. Travel and tourism can be very beneficial for the economy of a country, especially a developing country, but it can also be damaging culturally and ecologically. However, the ability to 'give back' through voluntary service while travelling helps the host country in many ways. An international demand for cultural programmes incites employment and volunteer/participant fees provide funding for the project infrastructure. Volunteers provide labour that may not otherwise be affordable as well as additional funding for research, reconstruction, and community development projects, etc., but they also bring a message of international goodwill and heighten cultural awareness, especially among the youth. Cultural programmes that teach volunteers indigenous languages, arts, folklore, dance, music, etc., are invaluable in preserving cultural heritage, not only for foreign study but especially for local pride and enthusiasm to continue passing along these cultural keystones to future generations.

Locally, in their own countries or communities, volunteers can also provide a public demand and the necessary physical or monetary resources for important research to be undertaken. Enthusiasts can get involved with local or national societies that hold lectures, publish newsletters and journals, organise excursions, and launch archaeological fieldwork investigations. Many projects provide students with an opportunity to gain field experience or thesis material while becoming involved in important scientific research efforts. And non-students may be interested in educational or alternative travel and contributing their energies to a worthy cause.

VOLUNTEER PROJECTS AND ORGANISATIONS

Until recently, volunteer opportunities were mainly offered by large organisations but the costs/fees charged limited the number of people who could afford them and participate. However, there are many smaller projects with a constant shortage of funding that greatly need volunteers. Often the contributions made by volunteers can maintain projects for years. This guide aims to introduce prospective volunteers to the many valuable projects throughout the world in need of volunteer assistance.

Voluntary organisations are often directed at people interested in alternative vacation. Many of the projects are aimed at youth but there are a considerable number who accept all ages, including retired people, with or without skills or a background in archaeology.

Museum associations take volunteers for administrative, public outreach work and sometimes take volunteers to assist in the laboratory and with associated fieldwork. There are regional and national museum associations throughout the world. A simple internet search will provide an extensive list (see Useful Websites).

Universities with well-established departments of anthropology or archaeology offer training courses or coordinate PhD projects requiring field staff. Participants pay tuition for credit and often must pay auditing fees for non-credit participation. The tuition is paid to the facilitating university but credit must be approved through the home institution of the student.

Independent research projects with established or inter-government organisations offer outreach programmes. Funding or (non-monetary) assistance may be provided by municipal or regional governments or on a national level.

Non-Government Organisations (NGOs) are typically non-profit and self-sufficient in the sense that they receive no funding from government agencies. They are strongly dependant upon public contributions and volunteer support.

Workcamps (International workcamp associations) organise voluntary projects for young participants, from all over the world, and in collaboration with local authorities. They are the ideal setting for young people or volunteers with no previous experience not wanting to commit too much time. They are therefore particularly suitable for students and young people as a meaningful way to spend a summer vacation or visit a new country or take part in a cultural exchange. Workcamp experience could be considered more of an alternative vacation than a true volunteering commitment. Nevertheless workcamps offer a good introduction to volunteering, and they are an enriching life experience for the work accomplished and for meeting people from many different countries and cultures who share the same interests and lifestyle.

Often no previous experience is required for workcamps; the structure is organised to lodge and cater to a certain number of volunteers, the tasks to be accomplished are simple, and the work is never in extreme situations. Often the only requirement is to know the language of the workcamp (most often English). For these reasons the workcamps are preferred by young people and students. Older volunteers may also be accepted but they should first verify that the type of work involved is of interest and within physical capabilities and know the average age of the other volunteers, in order not to feel too isolated from the rest of the group. More experienced volunteers can always apply for a coordinating position.

Workcamps and unpaid volunteer positions obviously have less competition but they may not be able to take volunteers with little notice because if the camp is popular the few available positions may already be filled. They may also require specific qualifications to meet the needs of the association or project at that particular time. And even though volunteers may be financially self-supporting and willing to work, they still require considerable engagement on the part of the organisation. Organisations often take only a limited number of volunteers since they require space, attention, coordination, assistance, transportation, and they must be provided with higher standards of hygiene and safety than what may be normally found in that country. It is advisable to make as large a search spectrum as possible to increase the chance of finding an organisation that is not only interested but also ready to accept a prospective volunteer to their project.

The following is a list of some of the organisations that coordinate international workcamps. Several already listed in the Guide are: Alliance of European Voluntary Service Organisations, CCIVS, Chantiers Jeunesse, Compagnons Batisseurs, Concordia, Elix Conservation Volunteers Greece, Cotravaux, FIYE, NICE, Jeunesse et Réconstruction, SCI, UNESCO, Volunteers for Peace, and YAP.

AFSAI started as one of the Italian partners of EVS and regularly organises workcamps in the sectors of community development, culture, education, etc. See: www.afsai.it.

AJED organises different activities for young people in Burkina Faso and Senegal such as workcamps, stays with guest families, and education programmes. The workcamps promote cultural exchanges. See: www.ajed.africa-web.org.

AJUDE was born during the post civil-war period in Mozambique when the region faced deep transformations. Workcamps involve community development, constructions, education, human rights, and women's issues. See: www.ajude.org.mz.

AVSO (Association of Voluntary Service Overseas) organises international workcamps in culture, education, community development, etc., for European Union residents. See: **www.avso.org**.

BWCA (Bangladesh Work Camps Association) organises national and international workcamps, study tours, international youth exchange, and leadership training on issues proclaimed by UNESCO towards establishing world peace. See www.mybwca.org.

Council Exchanges USA runs international volunteer projects for Americans to work overseas on projects on cultural, construction, community development, etc. See www.councilexchanges.org.

Eurocultura organises cultural exchanges and youth workcamps throughout Europe. See: www.eurocultura.it.

EVS (European Voluntary Service) offers a contact point between other workcamp or volunteer associations and volunteers and is a reference for National agencies working in close collaboration with the European Commission. See: ec.europa.eu/youth.

Inventaire des monuments et chantiers is a French workcamp organisation; they also have a Guide Book for work camps. See: http://cvmclubduvieuxmanoir.free.fr/club/inventaire_chantiers.php.

Jeunesse et Réconstruction (see listing) is an organisation for volunteer camps and activities abroad and in France in reconstruction, renovation, and conservation. See: http://www.volontariat.org.

Solidarités Jeunesses is related to the Minister of Youth and Sport in France and is the French branch of YAP. It organises international camps in the world for long- and short-term voluntary service. See: http://www.solidaritesjeunesses.org/.

Voluntary Service International (VSI) Africa/Asia/Latin America Exchange programme enables Irish people and people from other European countries to gain an insight and understanding of developing countries by participating in voluntary workcamps organised by local voluntary/community organisations working as part of a group of international volunteers alongside local volunteers and villagers on projects of a practical nature, such as building a school or health clinic, planting trees, or repairing village roads. See: http://www.vsi.ie/.

Volunteer Africa lets volunteers work with villagers on projects and get involved in village life. See: www.volunteerafrica.org.

HOW TO START

Tips for Contacting an Organisation

Having a copy of *Archaeo-Volunteers* has been the first step. Below are some suggestions to help you find the organisation most suited to your interests and be accepted on their project.

Have clear in mind what you want to do, the subject you prefer, the geographical location, the duration of your volunteering period, and the costs you can afford. This will help you select and reduce the number of organisations you need to apply to. If you are professionally qualified in a specific field, and you think that your skills may be useful, look specifically for organisations in your sector where you would best be able to use your qualifications. Conversely, do not consider organisations that do not need your skills. Select a list of organisations and divide them into priorities and start contacting both groups systematically.

Use the fastest possible method to contact an organisation. Remember that interesting projects or organisations also have many applicants, and they usually fill their available positions on a first come, first serve basis. Therefore, you want to be as fast as possible in letting them know that you are interested in taking a position with them. Do not lose time by sending a letter by regular mail, unless you are required to do so, but immediately start sending e-mails, even if only as preliminary enquiries. E-mail is usually a good way to make a first contact with an organisation and get to know who they are without being too committed. It is also a good idea to verify before applying whether or not you have a good chance to be accepted. If not, do not waste time, go on to the next organisation on your list. Should you not receive a reply within 3-5 days, be prepared to send reminders or telephone to confirm their e-mail address or verify whether or not it is worth continuing your application process with them, particularly if it requires filling out lengthy forms.

If an organisation is in a developing country, make it easy for them to respond to you. Remember that organisations in poorer countries often are short of funds. Therefore, help them by enclosing self-addressed stamped envelopes should you exchange regular mail (for example you may need an original letter in their stationary paper to obtain the Visa). Always enclose one or more international postal reply coupon as a form of courtesy, even if you are not required to do so. Remember, if you interact with a large organisation, well-equipped for recruiting volunteers, they will have all the means to contact you.

Contact many organisations to select an organisation, or a specific project, well in advance. Properly planning your vacation or time in advance will allow you to find the best airfares and select the best period suitable to you. Get detailed information on what to expect: the type of work, accommodation, food, climate, clothing, equipment necessary, etc. Owing to a lack of space this information cannot be included in the projects' description in this guide.

Research the history and culture of the subject of the project as well as the culture, customs, and climate of the host country. A basic understanding of archaeological techniques is a good idea for personal preparation but if no experience is required by the project, they will likely provide all the necessary training to give you the skills to work effectively and enjoyably. They should also confirm the project details, such as the living, working and safety conditions, prior to departure. Request contact information of previous volunteers and correspond with them to further verify the conditions of the projects.

This guide aims to give a general overview of a given organisation and give you tools to find many others. Never show up at a project location without having first applied and having been accepted and confirmed. Most projects have limited positions, lodging and personnel. Very rarely are they equipped to take on an unexpected volunteer. Unless very clearly stated by the project or organisation, never arrive at a project unannounced. It is disruptive, unprofessional, and awkward for the project leader. If you choose to inquire while already travelling in a certain area, do not be disappointed if you are rejected.

Application Advise

Do exactly what is required by an organisation for being accepted. If they require you to complete their application form, whether it is sent to you or whether you download it from their website, do fill it out, even if you have already submitted your detailed CV. If you apply with an organisation where the official language is not English but another major international language that you will be expected to use if accepted by them, send at least the cover letter in this language and be prepared to translate your CV if necessary. The competition to participate in some projects may be high. Treat your applications as you would a job application. In the application or on your CV state your skills: language, computer or web design, or artistic (e.g., for illustrating and photography) that may be useful to archaeological projects. State your educational background, elaborate if you have a relevant specialisation in the arts and sciences, and reference any previous volunteer experience you may have. Research projects associated with Universities may require only experienced volunteers or research assistants. Field positions such as these offer opportunities for graduate students to gain thesis material or practical field experience to advance them in their careers. Letters of recommendation or presentation from professors or recognised academics may be required.

Many organisations with workcamp programmes often request an advanced deposit or membership to their organisation. If accepted, do not be late in paying. Inquire about the fastest method to transfer funds: by international telegraph money order, credit card, and money wire from bank to bank, etc.

Preliminary meetings or training courses - attendance may not be feasible for international participants, but be sure to have this requirement waived if it is not possible to attend.

Prospective volunteers should exchange frequent e-mails, or even fax or phone calls, with project leaders and ensure that communication is always prompt and clear. Follow up upon the status of your application to make sure that it has been received and at what point in time you should expect to receive a response by.

WHAT TO BRING

Documentation to Bring

Necessary documentation includes passports, visas, permission clearance for some countries, and insurance (personal, medical, and travel) may or may not be included in the project fees (see below for further details on insurance). Make photocopies of all important documentation and leave one set with an emergency contact at home and carry another set with you, separate from the originals, as a back-ups in case you lose the originals. Carry on you, and provide to the organisation you are joining, the name of a person to contact in case of emergency. Be sure that your family or your friends know exactly where you are going and for how long. Give them the information for where you can be contacted or found in case of emergency.

If you intend to travel abroad to a country requiring extensive visas and permissions, begin all the documentation acquisitions at least six months prior to your departure. When in transit or in non-secure areas keep your money, passport and important documents in a purse or small sack under your clothing, even when sleeping, or at arm's reach and eye's view when bathing. Do not put all your resources in one place. Divide your money and other resources and stash them in different bags and clothing.

Passport: Up to date and valid for at least six months beyond your intended stay abroad. Carry the original in a secure place. Keep one copy separate from the original as a back-up while travelling and another left at home with an emergency contact.

Visas: It is often necessary to have either a tourist or student visa to enter a foreign country or to participate in a study or research project. It may take several months to apply for the visa, in which case make sure that you have initiated the bureaucratic process enough in advance, or the visa may be purchased in the airport upon arrival, like a form of tax - in this case ensure you have the money on you to pay for it and local currency may be the only option. Information concerning visa requirements is usually provided from the project or organisation you will be joining, but you should also consult the embassy or consulate of the country of destination in your home country.

Currency: Bring small amounts of local currency (enough to cover you for a couple of days of room, board, and local travel upon arrival) and the remainder of your resources in the form of traveller's cheques. The exchange rate may not be as favourable in this method, but the security against loss or theft is worth the cost. Keep sound records of the traveller's checks that you have already used. Bring a bank card that works internationally and possibly a credit card (carry the international emergency phone number with you to cancel the card in case of loss or theft).

Insurances: Travel, medical, and personal/life insurances are highly recommended and may be necessary. There may be special rates available to students and seniors. Even if the organisation you are joining has insurance, it is better to have your own personal policy as well in case of any litigation. Have insurance that covers theft, lost of luggage, flight delay or cancellation, emergency evacuation, change of return flight, and emergency health coverage for ambulance, hospital, and medication. If you are a citizen of a European Union (EU) country and you will be attending a project in another EU country, request an E111 form from your National Health Service, which will qualify you for coverage by the health system of the host country. If you have an insurance against theft, have receipts at home of any valuable you are taking with you and if this is not possible take photographs of the items. Keep receipts of things that you purchase while travelling.

Vaccination card: Carry a vaccination card (stating current vaccinations stamped from the medical board where the vaccinations were taken) and health card stating your blood type and any allergies you may have. Inquire at the relevant embassy for vaccination requirements. Realise that certain vaccinations or preventative medications, such as anti-malarial drugs, must be started at least a couple of weeks before entering the country that hosts the risk. Obviously, most precautions only apply to visiting developing or tropical countries, but almost all projects that involve excavation work require an anti-tetanus and possibly a hepatitis vaccination.

Clothing and Equipment to Bring

Always request a detailed list of clothing and equipment that is required to bring to the project. Most projects will supply the heavy and technical equipment and safety gear such as hard hats. Volunteers may need to purchase a personal trowel in advance (not riveted and no greater than 4 inches/10cm long) to bring for their own use. Bring a measuring tape, water bottle, alarm clock, flashlight, batteries, and sunglasses. Various types footwear may be required: steel-toed boots for certain work settings or soft flat-soled shoes for delicate areas with artefacts being photographed in-situ. Kneeling pads and gardening gloves are recommended.

Clothing must be climate appropriate and protective against sun, wind, or rain. Comfort is very important. Tight or restrictive clothing will make excavation work difficult. Bring sufficient clothing to last with limited laundry possibilities but do not over pack as you may be responsible to carry your supplies between various locations and space may be limited. Bring a hat suitable for the climate in which you will be working (sun, rain, cold, etc.). Raingear should include jacket and pants, hat, and perhaps even rubber boots.

Bring all necessary medical and personal hygiene supplies. A personal first aid kit is advisable and include within it sunscreen, insect repellent, and other items to deal with skin concerns: cuts, scrapes, rashes, bug bites, burns, slivers, blisters, etc., especially if you will be joining a workcamp or an excavation project. If travelling overseas, it may be a good idea to take a medical and dental examination prior to your trip to help ensure against any medical problems while away.

If the project is a camp setting, you may be required to bring your own tent, sleeping bag and mat, cutlery, etc.

Some final suggestions on what to bring include a regional travel guide and a personal journal describing the work you are doing, camp life, your impressions of the local culture, etc., by which to remember your experience by years later.

USEFUL WEBSITES

The World Wide Web is the most comprehensive source of information on voluntary work worldwide. Most of the websites of the organisations listed in this guide provide good links, however, the following pages highlight the most useful websites to help the prospective volunteer find opportunities in archaeology, anthropology, palaeontology, etc. Recommended books include The International Directory of Voluntary Work by Crimson Publishing (London, UK) listing thousands of voluntary placements worldwide in different sectors including archaeology and related fields; and directly in the field of archaeology the Archaeological Fieldwork Opportunities Bulletin is one of the best guides and is published by the Archaeological Institute of America (see website next page).

The following list offers a variety of useful websites and is a sampling from the links page of the ArchaeoVolunteers website, accessible only to those who have purchased this Guide (see page 3), which is updated periodically. The to find the links page you must enter with your User ID and Password:

http://www.archaeovolunteers.org

The Internet allows rapid access to information from almost anywhere in the world on practically every subject. The organisations involved with volunteers are certainly a primary use of the Internet. Non-profit organisations in developing countries have little funding and considerable demand for communicating their calls for assistance, fundraising, public awareness campaigns, volunteers, and other needs. After choosing a sector of interest, the type of work, the country of destination, etc., the Internet becomes a great tool for prospective volunteers to find the most suitable project. Search-engines, links to other sites, and organisation newsletters are valuable tools for researching volunteer opportunities and finding associations either close to home or in a specific country. Use a good search engine and look for "association + volunteering + the city/country name" to find nearby associations. To find workcamps type in the key word "workcamp" and the country name. The volunteer positions are typically listed in the menu under "Get involved!" or "Join us". Most often, after a section dedicated to fundraising, there is a section concerning volunteering.

About.com: Archaeology

Articles and directory of Internet sites, including a world atlas of archaeology on the web, and excellent links.
http://archaeology.about.com

Archaeological Institute of America (AIA)

North America's oldest and largest organisation devoted to the world of archaeology. Members include professional archaeologists, students, and enthusiasts from the US, Canada, and overseas. They publish annually the Archaeological Fieldwork Opportunities Bulletin listing fieldwork opportunities also with a searchable online database.
www.archaeological.org

Passport In Time

Passport in Time (PIT) is a volunteer archaeology and historic preservation programme of the USDA Forest Service (FS). The website lists many fieldwork opportunities and environimental/heritage conservation projects in the US.
www.passportintime.com

Archaeology Fieldwork

An online forum that offers employment listings, academic resources, many discussion boards, and general information.
www.archaeologyfieldwork.com

I Love The Past

A website dedicated to viewing and reviewing historic houses, castles, museums and archaeology fieldwork around Britain and abroad. Made by the Current Archaeology magazine team, is very updated and full of excavation opportunities.
www.ilovethepast.com

Past Horizons

A huge listing of archaeologic projects abroad, an online magazine, videos, podcast news, an archaeology tool store and more.
www.pasthorizons.com/WorldProjects/

Shovelbums

US archaeology employment resource with thousands of registered members on the moderated employment announcement mailing list.
www.shovelbums.org

Archaeology Digs
A blog about many aspects of archaeology, with listings of archaeological digs, job opportunities, field schools, archaeological travel tours and more.
www.archaeologydigs.blogspot.com

Archaeology Magazine Links
Links section of the Archaeology Magazine with a comprehensive listing of all branches of archaeology.
www.archaeology.org/wwwarky

Pastscape
English Heritage website intended to supply archaeological and architectural information to the public by searching nearly 400,000 records.
http://pastscape.org.uk/

ArchaeoBlog
A Weblog with archaeology-news from all around the world in English and German.
www.acagle.net/ArchaeoBlog

Fasti On Line
A database of archaeological excavations since 2000 in the Mediterranean area.
www.fastionline.org

BBC - Archaeology
The BBC page about archaeology with many useful resources.
www.bbc.co.uk/history/archaeology/

ArchaeoSpain
Offers fieldwork opportunities and college credit at various Spanish excavation sites.
http://archaeospain.com/programs.htm

British Archaeological Jobs & Resources
A source for jobs in the archaeological field, with news, directories, databases, etc.
www.bajr.org

Archaeologica
Weekly podcast program about what's new in archaeology news. Wide links page for recent archaeological news.
www.archaeologica.org

Amazing Worlds of Archaeology, Anthropology, and Ancient Civilizations
Resource for students and others interested in the fields of archaeology,
anthropology, and ancient civilisations divided by topic.
www.archaeolink.com

Anthropology Resources on the Internet
Anthropology directory of academic to amateur level. Projects, associations,
and relevant resources with focus on academic objectivity. In French.
www.archeodroit.net

Archaeologic.com
Directory of fieldwork opportunities and other relevant resources.
http://archaeologic.com/fieldwork_directory.htm

Archaeological Research Resources
Internet directory maintained by Historic Archaeological Research of history
and archaeology websites, including organisations, directories, technical
references, and online publications.
www.har-indy.com/Links.html

Archaeology: An Introduction
Links to web resources, archives, and documents about archaeology for
students and enthusiasts.
www.staff.ncl.ac.uk/kevin.greene/wintro/

Archaeology Channel
Archaeology and related subjects presented through streaming media by
the Oregon-based Archaeological Legacy Institute. Videos can be viewed
online and purchased.
www.archaeologychannel.org

Archaeology Info
Significant archaeological discoveries on human origins. Illustrated and
referenced descriptions of hominids. Articles, images, bookstore, and links.
www.archaeologyinfo.com

Archaeology Pages
Archaeology related articles covering archaeo-geology, prehistory, palaeoanthropology, the Andes, Meso-America, American Southwest and rock art.
www.jqjacobs.net/anthro

Archeologia Italiana
Archaeology in Italy with links, a discussion forum (in Italian), information on excavations, etc.
www.archeologia.com/links

ArchNet
Archaeology section of the World Wide Web Virtual Library.
http://archnet.asu.edu

Athena Review Guide to Archaeology on the Internet
Primary information on archaeology and history. Combination of graphic images and online sources and databases.
www.athenapub.com/inet/guide2.htm

Bosco's Rockpile
Recreational site of interest in archaeology, geology, and palaeontology. Links to related sites, photos, information, and digs in the USA.
www.boscarelli.com/where2dig.htm

BuildingConservation.Com
Online information centre for the conservation and restoration of historic buildings, churches, and garden landscapes.
www.buildingconservation.com

Ciudad Virtual de Antropologia y Arqueologia
A portal of archaeology in Spanish.
www.arqueologia.com.ar - http://www.antropologia.com.ar
www.naya.org.ar

Council for British Archaeology
Principal UK-wide NGO promoting knowledge, appreciation, and care of the historic environment. British Archaeology, published six times a year, contains the CBA Briefing produced by the British Archaeological Information Service with information on excavations and fieldwork, conferences, lectures, events, book reviews, and announcements.
www.britarch.ac.uk

Cultural Heritage Search Engine
Search engine about the conservation of cultural heritage, restoration, and maintenance of architecture and preservation of urban landscapes.
www.culturalheritage.net

Current Archaeology
British archaeological bi-monthly magazine referencing archaeological resources, digs, discoveries, events, and camps throughout the UK.
www.archaeology.co.uk

EARP - European Archaeological Research Project
Database for excavation opportunities on the Internet.
http://archweb.LeidenUniv.nl/archeonet/fieldwork_oppor.html

European Association of Archaeologists
Membership-based association open to all archaeologists and other related or interested individuals or organisations worldwide working in prehistory, classical, medieval, and later archaeology: academics, environmental and field archaeologists, heritage managers, historians, museum curators, conservators, underwater archaeologists, etc.
www.e-a-a.org

Institute of Cultural Affairs Worldwide
Non-profit organisation working on cultural programmes worldwide for individual, community, and organisational development. Highly participatory programmes in collaboration with other public, private, voluntary, or local community organizations.
www.ica-international.org

Institute of Field Archaeologists
Professional organisation for archaeologists in the UK promoting professional standards and ethics for conserving, managing, understanding, and promoting enjoyment of the heritage. Information for archaeologists, students, and purchasers of archaeological services.
www.archaeologists.net

Institute of Nautical Archaeology
Non-profit scientific and educational organisation looking for and excavate archaeologically important maritime sites in the world and disseminating this knowledge through scholarly and popular publications, seminars, and lectures as well as assisting the professional training and education of future nautical archaeologists through their participation in Institute projects.
http://ina.tamu.edu/

Into Archaeology
Resources for professionals and enthusiasts including software, articles, book reviews, news, multimedia, and specialised editor reviewed channels.
www.intoarch.com

Marshalltown Trowel Company
Large manufacturer of masonry and related hand tools.
www.marshalltown.com

Prehistory.org
Large website is a collection of links in various sectors with strong emphasis
on archaeology and its related disciplines.
www.prehistory.org/links.htm

Society for American Archaeology
International organisation dedicated to research, interpretation, and
protection of archaeological heritage of the Americas. Members include
professionals, students, and vocational archaeologists working in
government agencies, universities, museums, and the private sector.
www.saa.org

Underwater Archaeology Discussion List
Link list of the archives of sub-archaeology of the University of Arizona.
http://lists.asu.edu/archives/sub-arch.html

Underwater Archaeology
Museums, shipwrecks, and projects.
www.pophaus.com/underwater/museums.html

World Archaeological Congress
Seeks to promote interest in the past of all countries and encourage the
development of regionally based histories and international academic
interaction.
www.worldarchaeologicalcongress.org

Links to Museum Associations:

American Association of Museums
Focal point for professionals in museum and museum-related fields.
www.aam-us.org

Australian Archaeological Association
Largest archaeological organisation in Australia with excellent links.
www.australianarchaeologicalassociation.com.au

Canadian Museums Association
Non-profit museums, art galleries, science centres, aquaria, archives, sports halls of fame, artist-run centres, zoos, and historic sites.
www.museums.ca

Museums Association of Great Britain
Official Museums Body in the UK, with information, up to date news, events and a monthly debate topic.
www.museumsassociation.org

Museum Security Network
Internet service and mailing list for museum security professionals, curators, librarians, registrars, specialised police, journalists, collectors, galleries, national parks, archaeologists, universities, and students.

RESPONSIBLE TOURISM

Responsible tourism deserves a separate mention. Indeed, it is not volunteering, but as the term suggests, "tourism made on tiptoe". The tourist tries to understand the local culture, to live with the locals, and to visit their villages, schools, farms, and cooperatives using the services offered by the local communities as much as possible so that they may increase their revenues. Responsible tourism is for those who want to travel, understand, and to be as little trouble to their host as possible. Several NGOs, in fact, are beginning to organise trips to the locations where their projects are carried out, so that the travellers may visit the volunteers and the communities being helped. Responsible tourism, in the context of this Guide, may be considered a gradual approach or introduction to volunteering.

HOW TO READ THE GUIDE

Archaeo-Volunteers is a directory. It lists organisations of many different sectors offering volunteer opportunities. The guide gives examples of the different kinds of opportunities but it cannot be considered comprehensive. If an organisation of interest cannot be found among the organisations listed, the section dedicated to resources on the Internet gives the reader the possibility of finding hundreds or thousands of additional organisations or projects. Organisations and projects are listed in alphabetical order. At the end of the Guide, there is an index with an Analytical Table listing the entries by the geographical area and period.

Meaning of Abbreviations

Where available, each entry in the Guide has listed:

The **address** and the **telephone** and **fax** numbers with the international codes. The local area code changes according to the country's telephone system. For example, to call the UK prefixed with the country and area code ++44 (20), calling from the UK do not dial ++44 (the international code) but add 0 (zero) before 20 (the local area code). Calling from Europe add 00 before 44 to call the UK, whereas from the US only dial 011 (the international code from the US to Europe) followed by 44.

E-mail and World Wide Web (**www**) addresses. Some organisations do not have a website: it can be useful to ask via e-mail or telephone if they have implemented one since the printing of this guide. If not, a prospective volunteer with good computer skills can help this organisation to make one; it is a good way to begin volunteering and an excellent introduction to the organisation. Organisations who do not have a website, and therefore do not have their e-mail address linked to a domain name, tend to change their e-mail address quite often. If, after a reasonable number of solicitations, an organisation does not answer to the e-mail messages, or a message bounces back, search for the project on the Internet to see if a new website has been established with new contact information. It is also possible to send an e-mail message to an organisation from the same country or of the same sector, which probably knows the organisation in question.

The reader should realise that projects are dynamic and details such as costs, accommodations, project duration, season dates, or countries in which the organisations operate may vary from year to year. New projects arise and old projects may end. Periodic verification of the websites of interest is highly recommended.

Desc.:   The description outlines the activities and objectives of the organisation or the project details including information about the site, the history, the research ambitions, or other details.

Per.:   The historical period to which the remnants that are excavated, studied, or restored belong to are defined. As much as possibile, these definitions have been left as defined by the projects and organisations themselves and therefore do not fall into a rigid categorisation set by this guide. For organisations with cultural projects not involved with excavation or restoration 'modern' or 'contemporary' has been written. Considering that the Period is an important component in selecting a project to participate in, an Analytical Table of Geographic Areas and Periods has been provided (see page 226) to easily find the projects or organisations working on a particular subject or in a particular area. Period definitions are found on page 34.

Country: The country or countries the project or organisation works in is stated. Larger organisations may run several projects in more than one country or worldwide. In these cases their projects and locations may change year to year and prospective volunteers should always confirm that the project they are interested in is still running in any particular country. The head office may be in a different country from that of the project.

Loc.:   The project location is a smaller, more specific reference than country. The city or village may be named or if the project is rural, a general geographic region may be explained.

Travel: Logistics for a meeting point for an international group is often difficult to assign and quite often the details of the travel arrangements are provided to the volunteers after their application has been approved. Often the volunteers will be picked up at a specified airport or bus or train station or are given instructions on how to arrive at the project site from these points. Always confirm prior to departure to a project whether there will be a pick-up arranged. If there is no pick-up, confirm the travel instructions and when you are to arrive at the project site.

Dur.:   The duration of the volunteer or study period is the minimum length of stay and the months or the season in which the project is running. Longer periods of stay beyond what is specified may be possible if the project is ongoing upon approval from the project or organisation or if space permits. Typically the minimum stay is two weeks to have the time to efficiently apply new skills from training; single day digs are also common for all ages; six weeks are standard for University credited courses. Field projects are usually in the summer months.

Age: The minimum age accepted is stated. Typically this is 18 years of age. Younger volunteers may be accepted with permission but often must be accompanied by a guardian. Several projects have programmes for families, school groups, and teenagers and are usually day or weekend events. There are usually no upper age restrictions stated but older volunteers must be comfortable with the physical demands of the project as all volunteers must be aware of their personal stamina and capabilities regardless of age.

Qualif.:   Any necessary qualifications or experience required by the volunteer is stated. Usually no experience is necessary however some professional digs may only accept students seeking course credit or field experience or professionals as experienced crew members or research collaborators.

Work: The type of work, such as excavation, survey, or laboratory work, is described as well as the work hours and days per week.

Lang.: Typically the language of the projects are in English or the language of the host country. It is important that the volunteer has the necessary language skill requirements to successfully participate in the project.

Accom.: The style and availability of accommodation varies greatly from project to project. Often excavation projects are in a camp setting. Volunteers may or may not have to provide their own camping gear (tent, sleeping bag, mat, etc.), and the availability of running and hot water, electricity, flush toilets may not exist. In camp settings understand prior to your arrival what the accommodation and field standards are and if you are comfortable with them. It is not unlikely to be in a field situation where there is no running or hot water and only outhouses or squat toilets. There is a wide range of hygiene facilities available from project to project. In some instances, showers (or makeshift saunas) are arranged but they may be as rare as once per week. Bathing may only be possible in a lake or a river. However, some projects house the participants in hotels or homes with all the modern comforts available and the worksite may also have a high infrastructure annex of buildings fully equipped with heating, plumbing, and electricity. The excavation site may even be situated in the middle of a large, modern city. Volunteers may be housed in dormitories, schoolhouses or other such buildings, hostels, hotels, motels, or bed and breakfasts, or be billeted by local families. Accommodation may not be provided but may provide suggestions for conveniently located and affordable options.

Cost: Project fees range from a small membership fee or project contribution to full room and board charges to complete travel package costs. If there is no fee, there are likely no benefits and the volunteer must be totally self-sufficient. Often the total cost stated is what covers the minimum or complete volunteer period. Some projects have introduced a very useful 'progressively decreasing cost' policy, depending on the length of stay. The rationale is that the longer a volunteer stays with a project, the more useful he or she becomes because of the experience gained. Always bring a reasonable amount of spending or emergency money in more than one form (local and home currency, a credit card, traveller's checks, or other).

Applic.: The first step in applying to a project or organisation should be to consult the website if one exists. Many websites for volunteer projects have an online form with which to apply. If application instructions are not provided, e-mail or telephone for a fast understanding of volunteer opportunities and then request further application instruction.

Notes: Additional information is provided when necessary, such as availability of academic credit, additional contacts, pertinent project details, what to bring, warnings or advice, etc.

See also: Related projects or organisations in the Guide are cross-referenced. If an organisation has project featured elsewhere in the guide, the names of these projects will be cited. These projects in turn will then reference the organisation. If two or more projects are related but there is no listing of their common organisation, the projects will cross-reference each other.

Analytical Table by Geographic Areas and Periods
Definitions

The Classification of projects by cultural/historical periods is difficult and often debatable between historians and archaeologists. Moreover, every civilisation (in different geographical areas) has its own historic period definitions. Therefore, in order to help the reader easily find projects or organisations in their preferred subject and area, the Guide provides an **Analytical Table of Geographical Areas and Periods** (see page 226) where the periods are subdivided for the purposes of the index. These definitions are not to be regarded as an academic resource but simply as a tool in reading the guide. Please excuse any errors, inaccuracies, misinterpretations, or lack of information within the Table or the referenced projects. The geographical area is obviously more comprehensible and more detailed information may be found on the possible website of any given project to help better historically locate a project of interest.

The categories are defined as follows:

Europe - Prehistory: encompasses from about the Palaeolithic (c. 100,000 years BP) to the Neolithic (c. 8,000 BC) to the Bronze Age c. 800 years BC.

Europe - Classic/Iron Age: from c. 800 BC to the birth of Christ. It includes the Greek Classic period, early Italian civilisations, such as the Etruscan, and the early expansion of the Roman Republic in the Mediterranean. In Northern Europe this period can be generally defined as the Iron Age.

Europe - Roman: starts approximately at the birth of Christ, when the Roman Empire started its expansion in Europe (for example with the invasion of Britain in 43). The Roman period ends approximately in the years between 450 and 550 with barbarian invasions.

Europe - Early Medieval: from approximately the end of the Roman Empire in the year 500 in Western Europe, a period of crisis without a dominant culture follows and lasts approximately to the year 1000.

Europe - Medieval: by the year 1000 in Europe a clear subdivision starts between centres of power - France, England, and Germany. During this period, the Crusades take place. Art and literature begin to flourish and reach their highest peak at the Renaissance after the year 1400.

Europe - Renaissance/Post Medieval: between 1400 and 1500. In Italy the Renaissance flourishes. The discovery and colonisation of the New World by other European countries begins.

Europe - Early Modern: from 1600 to 1800; from the Baroque Age to about the time of the French Revolution.

Europe - Modern: from 1800 to World War II, this period sees the growth of industrial societies, the beginning and end of large colonial empires and two World Wars.

Europe - Contemporary: this period considers the Art and Architecture after WWII.

Europe - Multiperiod: this definition includes organisations with different projects that encounter different layers in the excavation relating to successive periods.

Middle East - Prehistory: corresponds approximately to European Prehistory, from the Palaeolithic, c. 100,000 years BC, to the Iron Age, 500 years BC.

Middle East - Greek-Roman: the eastern shores of the Mediterranean were under the influence of what was happening on the Western shores between 300 BC and 500 AD; for simplicity this period has been classified in the Analytical Table as 'Greek-Roman'.

Middle East - Islamic/Medieval: in the year 700 the Islamic period starts and continues all the way to the Modern era. Christian architecture flourishes in the Medieval period in some countries, such as Armenia.

Asia - Prehistory: Far Eastern civilisations flourished from about 1000 BC. Prehistory can be considered to be belonging to the preceding periods.

Asia - Far East Civilisations: in China, Mongolia, Korea, and Japan history begins prior to 1000 BC. Although many periods (dynasties) can be identified among these important civilisations (just to name a few: the Qin, Han, Tang, and Song dynasties), for simplicity they have been grouped together.

Asia - Modern/Contemporary: grouped in this period are both the 19th and 20th centuries.

Africa - Prehistory/Palaeonthology: Africa saw the beginning of human evolution. Prehistory can be traced from about 3 million years BP to c. 2000 BC. For lack of space palaeonthological projects have been grouped in this category.

Africa - Modern/Contemporary: grouped mainly to consider cultural projects (such as projects on preserving traditional music or dances).

North America - Prehistory/Palaeonthology: from the early colonisation of the American continent by Asian populations, starting from about 20,000 years BP. For lack of space palaeonthological projects have been included in this group.

North America - Early Cultures: native American cultures were living undisturbed before the arrival of European colonists in 1600 on the East Coast and up to the early 1800s in the West. These cultures were well established from a few thousand years BC.

North America - Modern: this era corresponds approximately to the same period in Europe. The American Revolution in 1776 is animated by principles of freedom and democracy similar to those of the French Revolution in 1789.

Latin America - Maya/Precolombian: the Mayan civilisation flourished in central America from c. 500 BC to the arrival of the Spanish Conquistadores in 1500. The Maya period has been subdivided in pre-classic, classic and late classic; for simplicity, the Analytical Table does not refer to these periods.

Latin America - Pre-Inca/Inca: in South America the Inca empire flourished in the 15th century. Within this category projects related to earlier periods have been included for simplicity.

Latin America - Colonial/Modern: in Central America from 1500 to 1700 the Spaniards left beautiful examples of baroque religious architecture. Contemporary architecture has been included for simplicity.

Caribbean: referring to periods from 1492 to contemporary, including early colonialism, piracy, the slave trade, etc., up to the modern era.

Worldwide: organisations that have projects concentrating on various periods in several countries around the world are found in this category.

IMPORTANT NOTE AND WARNING

The Editor and Publisher of *Archaeo-Volunteers* has decided, both in order to offer prospective volunteers the widest possible choice and to be a valid historical preservation instrument, to cite, whenever possible, small projects and organisations, particularly in developing countries, for the following reasons:

1) Without *Archaeo-Volunteers* many small projects and organisations would not be able to receive volunteers from developed nations. We think that we should help as best as we can this historical preservation potential, particularly if it comes directly from local organisations, without an input from large organisations from our side of the world.

2) Prospective volunteers, by purchasing this guide, expect to find something different and unique from what is normally offered by large organisations in developed countries.

3) Often small projects require non-paying and long-term volunteers, which is what many of *Archaeo-Volunteers* readers expect. These opportunities are also usually offered at extremely affordable costs to the volunteers, which is not the case of projects offered from large organisations, which are often expensive and don't allow long-term volunteering.

Before joining projects and organisations, prospective volunteers should carefully read the following considerations and warnings:

1) **Because of obvious cost reasons,** which would then reflect on the cover price, **the Editor and Publisher cannot personally visit every project** listed in this guide but have to trust what projects and organisations (or the websites or previous volunteers) declare.

2) **Small projects and organisations,** particularly in developing countries, mainly because of shortage of funding or qualified personnel or because of conflicts with local populations and/or local authorities, **often change their programmes or even interrupt their activities without informing the Editor and Publisher of** *Archeo-Volunteers.*

3) Before joining a project volunteers should verify the validity of what **is declared** on the project website (if one exists) or in this guide.

4) Prospective volunteers should **exchange frequent e-mails,** or even fax or phone calls, **with project leaders** and ensure that communication is always prompt and clear. They should also confirm the project details, such as the living, working and safety conditions, prior to departure.

5) Prospective volunteers to any project should **ask names** and addresses **of previous volunteers and correspond with them** to further verify the conditions of the projects.

6) Volunteers should **never join a project by going directly to the location** without previous correspondence and verification of existing conditions.

7) Prospective volunteers should read carefully the WARNING on the third page of this book.

Good luck with your "archaeo-volunteering"!

ORGANISATIONS AND PROJECTS LIST

Aang Serian Peace Village

PO Box 2113
Arusha Tanzania
Tel.: ++255 (755) 744 992
E-mail: aang_serian@hotmail.com; enolengila@yahoo.co.uk
www.aangserian.org.uk

Desc.: Aang Serian (meaning 'House of Peace' in Maasai language) is an independent, non-profit organisation. It is officially registered with the National Arts Council of Tanzania as an organisation for the promotion of arts and culture. Aang Serian is now establishing itself as a global NGO dedicated to preserving indigenous traditions and knowledge and promoting intercultural dialogue around the world.

Per.: Modern/contemporary.

Country: Tanzania.

Loc.: Arusha.

Travel: Details provided upon application.

Dur.: 2 months to 1 year, depending on project.

Age: Minimum 18.

Qualif.: Non-professional volunteers with relevant skills to the project.

Work: Help to develop cultural programmes among local communities.

Lang.: English.

Accom.: Basic lodging.

Cost: Approximately US$1,385/2 months.

Applic.: References and a CV/resume will be required and a US$100 deposit is payable on application.

Achill Archaeological Field School

Achill Folklife Centre
Dooagh, Achill, County Mayo Ireland
Tel.: ++353 (098) 43564
Fax: ++353 (098) 43564
E-mail: info@achill-fieldschool.com
www.achill-fieldschool.com

Desc.:	Achill Archaeological Field School is involved in research excavations in the mountain of Slievemore on Achill Island, County Mayo. Academic credits are available for modular courses and are awarded by the National University of Ireland at Galway.
Per.:	Early Bronze Age. Historic Period sites.
Country:	Ireland.
Loc.:	Dooagh Village, Achill Island, County Mayo. Off the west coast of Ireland.
Travel:	Train from Dublin Heuston Station to Westport, then bus to Achill Island.
Dur.:	4-12 weeks; May to August.
Age:	Minimum 18.
Qualif.:	Students of archaeology, anthropology and related disciplines.
Work:	Excavation and survey on various sites on Slievemore mountain.
Lang.:	English.
Accom.:	Self-catered.
Cost:	EUR2,950-3,850.
Applic.:	Contact field school directly.

ADMAT — The Tile Wreck Maritime Archaeological Project (1720's)

Anglo-Danish Maritime Archaeological Team (ADMAT)
12 Penners Gardens, Langley Road, Surbiton, Surrey KT6 6JW UK
E-mail: maritime_archaeology@yahoo.co.uk;
info@admat.org.uk
www.admat.org.uk

Desc.:	This maritime archaeological survey and dig is of *The Tile Wreck*, where thousands of terracotta square floor tiles, shaped and pre-cut granite blocks, over 2,000 artefacts and many cannons and anchors were found. This site is among the most important in the country, and details in the lower hull provide great insight into ship construction of the late 1690s to early 1700s.
Per.:	Post Columbus; 1600-1700s.
Country:	Dominican Republic, Caribbean.
Loc.:	Monte Cristi on the north Coast of the Dominican Republic.
Travel:	From Santiago (STI) airport, 2hrs to Monte Cristi.
Dur.:	2 or 4 weeks; April to August.
Age:	Minimum 18.
Qualif.:	No experience necessary. Training in the principles and practice of maritime archaeology. Diving certification required for divers.
Work:	Maritime archaeology, survey and excavation.
Lang.:	English.
Accom.:	Room & board at the ADMAT Maritime Archaeological Centre in Monte Cristi. Shared bedrooms with bunk or camp beds and a bathroom with shower. Private hotel rooms are available nearby (not included in project cost). Lunch provided on the boat.
Cost:	GB£650; administration, room & board, tuition and local transport included. Airfare, travel, medical and diving insurances and personal expenses not included.
Applic.:	Online form on the web site www.admat.org.uk/tw1.htm. Application open to both divers and non-divers.

African Legacy

Department of Conservation Sciences
Bournemouth University
46a Ophir Road, Bournemouth, Dorset BH8 8LT UK
Tel.: ++44 (706) 796 3828 - Fax: ++44 (706) 796 7822
E-mail: african.legacy@gmail.com
http://apollo5.bournemouth.ac.uk/africanlegacy/

Desc.: Nigeria has more languages and ethnic groups than any other nation on earth, together with a visible archaeology including the world's longest ancient earthworks and earliest iron-smelting. This project involves surveys in rainforest and savannah, mapping new features, establishing Nigeria's first interactive museum, organising an archaeological library, aerial photos, satellite imagery, photography, pioneering and promoting new technologies (such as baobab tree dating), and liaising with other Nigerian institutions.

Per.: Whatever encountered: 2,400 BC to present.

Country: Nigeria.

Loc.: Covers much of Nigeria, using previous bases.

Travel: Fly to Lagos, then public transport elsewhere.

Dur.: Minimum 3 weeks are preferred; year round.

Age: Minimum 18.

Qualif.: No previous experience necessary. A positive attitude and a love of challenges required.

Work: On-the-job training in unorthodox, cost-effective Rapid Survey Techniques to map Nigeria's archaeology, cultural landscapes, and local histories. Each day there are different work options.

Lang.: English and over 400 Nigerian languages.

Accom.: Varies with project location.

Cost: GB£400/month, plus GB£50 contingency expenditure; airfare and visa (varies from GB£500-800) are not included. ASAP is available to facilitate travel organisation.

Applic.: Contact ASAP via e-mail, telephone or post.

AIEP — Association for Educational, Cultural and Work International Exchange Programs

28 Isahakyan Street, Room.22, Yerevan 0009 Armenia
Tel.: ++374 (10) 584 733
Fax: ++374 (10) 529 232
E-mail: aiep@arminco.com
www.aiep.am

Desc.:	AIEP sponsors historical restoration workcamps, technical internships, training and educational exchange programmes for students and youth in order to establish economic, cultural and educational connections between Armenia and other countries. This sample project is at Dilijan, one of the largest health-spa resorts in Armenia, within a national forest preserve with numerous historical monuments, the most interesting being the group of buildings of the Haghartsin Monastery.
Per.:	Medieval; 8th to 13th centuries.
Country:	Armenia.
Loc.:	Dilijan, about 62mi (100km) from Yerevan.
Travel:	Pick-up at Zvarnots airport and bus to workcamp.
Dur.:	15 days; July or August.
Age:	Minimum 18.
Qualif.:	No experience necessary.
Work:	Reconstruction of historic buildings and general cleaning. Monday to Friday; 4-5hrs/day.
Lang.:	English, Russian, Armenian.
Accom.:	The Holiday Hotels, near Dilijan and Ijevan. Some meals provided, others self-catered. Bring kitchen utensils and towels.
Cost:	EUR500 registration fee plus US$10 per diem. Room & board and transfers included. Personal expenses, travel and airport tax not included.
Applic.:	By e-mail. Deadline 8 weeks before project start date.

Alliance of European Voluntary Service Organisations

Secretariat c/o MS Denmark
Borgergarde 14, 1300 København Denmark
Tel.: ++45 (8619) 7766 - Fax: ++45 (8619) 7061
E-mail: alliance@alliance-network.eu
www.alliance-network.eu

Desc.: This International Non-Governmental Youth Organisation (INGYO) represents national organisations running international voluntary service projects. Each organisation promotes community development, intercultural education, understanding and peace through voluntary service. The Alliance consists of 43 member organisations from 27 countries. A workcamp involves 10-20 volunteers from 5-10 different countries. Projects take place in communities and provide volunteers the possibility to meet people from other countries and be hosted by the local community, thus gaining an intercultural experience while being a useful and active world citizen.

Per.: Modern, contemporary.

Country: Worldwide.

Loc.: Various.

Travel: Details provided upon application to specific project.

Dur.: Short-term projects last 2-3 weeks; in some cases, long-term projects last up to 12 months. Alliance members organise international workcamps throughout the year, mostly during the summer months.

Age: Minimum 18.

Qualif.: No experience necessary.

Work: Volunteers can engage in a wide variety of community development tasks, including environmental, construction, renovation, social, cultural and archaeological work.

Lang.: English or language of host country.

Accom.: Variable. May be group camping, dorms or hostels or billeting with host families.

Cost: Typically a membership or administration fee plus travel and personal expenses.

Applic.: International Volunteer Projects are organised in each country by a national Alliance member, which also recruits volunteers within that country. All Alliance members place only individuals residing in their own country on projects. Interested volunteers should therefore only contact their national Alliance member. The members also work closely with similar national and international organisations in Europe and worldwide. Individuals or organisations in other countries who would like to get involved should contact the Coordinating Committee for International Voluntary Service (see listing) at UNESCO in Paris to find out the name of the voluntary service organisation in their own country.

Alutiiq Museum & Archaeological Repository

Community Archaeology

215 Mission Road, Suite 101, Kodiak, Alaska 99615 USA

Tel.: ++1 (907) 486 7004

Fax: ++1 (907) 486 7048

E-mail: receptionist@alutiiqmuseum.org

www.alutiiqmuseum.org   *(find "education" on menu)*

Desc.:   Deposits are chosen to answer questions about Alutiiq prehistory while focusing on sites threatened by erosion, vandalism or modern development. Participants join in hands-on exploration of Alutiiq heritage and historic preservation. In 2000, this programme received the National Award for Museum Service.

Per.:   Prehistoric sites ranging from 7500 to 300 years old.

Country: United States.

Loc.:   Kodiak Island, in the Gulf of Alaska; sites in the Chiniak Bay area.

Travel: Island access by plane (taxi to town) or ferry (docks in town). Daily shuttle from museum at 8.30, returning from site at 17.30.

Dur.:   1 day (8hrs) to 6 weeks; July to August.

Age: Minimum 14.

Qualif.:   No experience necessary.

Work: Excavation, carrying and washing sediment, mapping and site cleaning. Washing, sorting and labelling artefacts, drying and organising samples, data entry and cleaning field gear. 4 weeks of fieldwork followed by 2 weeks of lab work; Monday to Friday.

Lang.:   English.

Accom.:   Not provided. Motels, B&Bs or camping available in Kodiak.

Cost: No fees. Tuition fees apply for academic credit. Room & board and personal expenses not included.

Applic.:   Contact museum archaeologist Patrick Saltonstall for programme dates, to schedule participation and for academic registration.

Notes: Bring rubber boots, raingear, gloves, kneeling pads and bug nets. Digging equipment provided.

Amphora Graveyard of Monte Testaccio

ArchaeoSpain
PO Box 1331
Farmington, Connecticut 06034 USA
Tel./Fax: ++1 (866) 932 0003
E-mail: programs@archaeospain.com
www.archaeospain.com/testaccio

Desc.: Participants will join a Spanish team analysing the epigraphy of the countless amphora remains which, after centuries of being tossed into the same spot, created a massive artificial mound in the centre of Rome. The notes written on the sherds make Testaccio the largest archive of Roman commerce in the world.

Per.: Roman.

Country: Italy

Loc.: Rome.

Travel: Meeting at the hotel on the first day. Travel from the airport is provided if necessary.

Dur.: September 20th to October 4th (dates have to be confirmed).

Age: Minimum 18.

Qualif.: No previous experience necessary.

Work: Although the schedule can change, the first week is usually dedicated to washing and sorting the finds. The second week is used for drawing, labelling, cataloguing and restoration.

Lang.: English; Spanish and Italian helpful. Participants will be immersed in the language daily, therefore it is hoped that they will take advantage and improve their spoken Spanish.

Accom.: Shared double rooms in a hotel. Meals at local restaurants.

Cost: US/Canada: US$2,915. Other countries: EUR2,160. Room and board, transportation from airport on the first day, application fee and administrative costs included. Travel expenses not included.

Applic.: Rolling.

Notes: Academic credit available with approval from home institution.

Anatolian Archaeology Field School

Purdue University, Study Abroad Program
Gazipasha, Turkey
Tel: ++90 (765) 496 6079
E-mail: rauhn@purdue.edu
http://web.ics.purdue.edu/~rauhn/fieldschool/field_index.htm;
www.studyabroad.purdue.edu/programs/

Desc.: This summer field opportunity is planned to furnish archaeological field experience for undergraduate student, who are exposed to the cultural heritage, history and field methods employed in Anatolian Archaeology and contemporary Turkish culture.

Per.: Prehistoric to Byzantine and Seljuk eras.

Country: Turkey.

Loc.: Gazipasha (Rough Cilicia); 12mi (20km) east of Alanya.

Travel: Flight from Istanbul to Antalya; then shuttle bus to Gazipasha.

Dur.: 1 month; July to August.

Age: Minimum 18, maximum 75 or older if fit.

Qualif.: No previous experience is necessary.

Work: The programme offers 6hrs credit (2 Purdue courses) for training in survey methodologies and technologies, Anatolian civilizations and actual field survey authorized by the Turkish government, field and laboratory instruction in systematic survey, field recording, photography, GPS locating, artefact analysis, architectural mapping, GIS mapping with satellite imagery. Travel to excavated sites nearby.

Lang.: English, Turkish, French.

Accom.: Lodging at air-conditioned hotel near the beach with swimming pool, cable TV and room with kitchenette; restaurants nearby.

Cost: Approximately US$4,200; registration, room, board and transportation included.

Applic.: Deadline for Turkish Research Application is November 30th annually. See website for details. Project director: Nicholas Rauh.

Ancient Metal Production and History in Southern Jordan

Univ. of CA, San Diego Archaeological Field School, Dpt. of Anthropology
9500 Gilman Drive, La Jolla, California 92093-0532 USA
Tel.: ++1 (858) 534 4145 - Fax: ++1 (858) 534 5946
E-mail: tlevy@weber.ucsd.edu
http://weber.ucsd.edu/Depts/Anthro/classes/tlevy/Fidan/

Desc.: This project occupies an area considered to be the gateway to one of the Levant's largest copper ore deposits. It provides an ideal open-air laboratory for studying the role of early copper ore extraction and metallurgy on the evolution of Levantine societies and involves archaeological survey along the Wadi al-Ghuwayb and excavation at the site of Khirbet en-Nahas, which has been known since early in the last century as among the largest Iron Age metal production sites in the Southern Levant. Students learn advanced on-site digital archaeology methods rooted in GIS (Geographic Information Systems).

Per.: Neolithic period to Iron Age; 11th to 5th centuries BC.

Country: Jordan.

Loc.: Edom Lowlands Region of southern Jordan, ca. 31mi (50km) south of the Dead Sea. Basecamp at the eastern end of the Wadi Fidan, at edge of the local Bedouin village of Qurayqira.

Travel: Fly to Amman airport (AMM). Group pick-up or travel instructions for travel to Faynan provided. The campsite lies at the end of a paved road that runs from the village of Qurayqira to the main Aqaba-Dead Sea Road. The road to Ain el-Fidan is well sign posted. Initial transportation into the site and a pick-up of the group flight will be provided.

Dur.: 10 weeks; late September to December.

Age: Minimum 18.

Qualif.: No experience necessary.

Work: Fidan Orientation; Dana Reserve Ecology Program; Field Survey of Wadi al-Ghuwayb; Excavation at Khirbet en-Nahas; Post-excavation.

Lang.:   English, Arabic.

Accom.:   Tent at the basecamp or a tent camp near to the site. Permanent structures provide a kitchen, toilets, showers and potable water. Camp beds with sleeping pads are provided but bring a personal sleeping bag or sleep sheets. A mosquito net is recommended. The tent camp has supplies transported in daily.

Cost: US$1,451 for 10 weeks plus US$150 registration fee. Tuition, room & board and local project related travel expenses included. Airfare and personal expenses not included. US$275 for the ecology field school (see Notes); tuition fees not included. Expect approximately a 20-30% increase in costs due to current economic difficulties. Students may earn 16 units of University of California, San Diego (UCSD) academic credit.

Applic.:   Online form. Submit the non-refundable registration deposit and application and fulfil the subsequent payment deadlines. Passport, visa and security forms also to be completed online. UCSD students must register through regular registration channels for the field school and the ecology course. Upon registration, an information packet will be sent. Limited to 40 students. Contact Dr. Thomas Levy for further details and instructions.

Notes: The Ecology Program is held in conjunction with the archaeology field school providing a background understanding of the desert ecology and environment of the region.

Aramus Excavations and Fieldschool

Department of Ancient History and Near Eastern Studies
University of Innsbruck
Langer Weg 11, 4. OG Austria
Tel.: ++43 (512) 376 58 /376 60 - Fax: ++43 (512) 376 98
E-mail: vai@uibk.ac.at
www.classicorient.at/aramus

Desc.: Aramus is an Urartian fortress occupied in the 1st millennium BC. A cuneiform inscription found nearby indicates a possible connection with the city of Darani, conquered by the Urartian King Argishti I in the 8th century BC. This project will shed light on the development and decline of the Urartu kingdom following social and political structures in the region. Subprojects focus on the research of a neolithic settlement in the Hatis region and an excavation will be done in the city of Aramus.

Per.: Urartu, Neolithic and Medieval Age.

Country: Armenia.

Loc.: Aramus, county Kotayk, Armenia; 9mi (15km) from Yerevan.

Travel: Flight via Vienna or Paris to Yerevan (EVN).

Dur.: 30 days; September.

Age: Minimum 18.

Qualif.: No experience necessary.

Work: On-site training covers the correct use of instruments and tools, identification and retrieval of stratigraphic units, examination and classification of finds, archaeological drawing, survey and mapping, graphical reconstruction, 3D scanning of architecture. Weekends are filled with excursions.

Lang.: German, English, Italian.

Accom.: Guest House of the Yerevan State University; half-board meals.

Cost: About EUR2,200 (students get a discount/grant) including flight, room, board, Visa, departure fee, bus transfer and excursions.

Applic.: Deadline for registration is May 1st. See website for details.

Archaeolink Prehistory Park

Oyne, Insch
Aberdeenshire AB52 6QP UK
Tel.: ++44 (1464) 851 500
Fax: ++44 (1464) 851 544
E-mail: interpret@archaeolink.co.uk
www.archaeolink.co.uk

Desc.: Archaeolink opened in 1997 to act as a link between the public and Aberdeenshire's rich archaeological heritage. A series of reconstructions (all based on archaeological evidence from northeast Scotland) form a Path through Prehistory. There are reconstructions from stone age camps through to a Roman Marching camp and an Iron Age farm.

Per.: Prehistory to Roman.

Country: United Kingdom.

Loc.: Insch, near Aberdeen.

Travel: The nearest train station is Insch, which is approximately 3mi (5km) from the centre; a regular bus service is also available from Inverurie and Aberdeen.

Dur.: 1 day to full season; March to October.

Age: Minimum 14 with guardian.

Qualif.: No experience necessary.

Work: Reconstruction.

Lang.: English.

Accom.: Local B&B or camping. Volunteers receive lunch and a variety of benefits in return for their support.

Cost: Volunteers must pay for their travel and room & board, but no contribution is required from the Park.

Applic.: Contact the park for further information.

Archaeological Excavations in Northern Spain

Department of Prehistory, Spanish Research Council CSIC
c/ Albasanz 26-28, Madrid 28037 Spain
Tel.: ++34 (916) 022 339 /(915) 221 416
Mob.: ++34 (626) 308 414 - Fax: ++34 (911) 304 5710
E-mail: acpinto@las.es; acpinto@ih.csic.es
http://accuca.conectia.es

Desc.:   Palaeolithic site excavation in the mountains of northern Spain.

Per.:   Palaeolithic.

Country: Spain.

Loc.:   Picos de Europa, Asturias (Spain).

Travel: Flight to Madrid or Bilbao, then by ALSA/EASA coach to Oviedo, then to the village of Cangas.

Dur.:   Minimum 4 weeks, maximum 8 weeks; July to August.

Age: Minimum 20.

Qualif.:   Archaeology/anthropology students or professionals with prior experience in excavations and lab work preferred; however, all committed applicants will be considered. Training provided.

Work: Excavation total station recording, collecting and processing finds and sediment. Work involves mountain hiking, often in wet weather and carrying sacks of sediment requiring physical stamina. Participants will be taken in a 4x4 vehicle to a drop-off point after which they will have a 20-min uphill hike in the mountains to the site and return again for pick-up at day's end. Monday to Saturday, 10hrs/day).

Lang.:   Spanish and/or English

Accom: Bunk beds in furnished houses, up to 6 people. Swimming pool.

Cost: EUR1,000/1 month, EUR1,500/full season, including room & board. Travel expenses not included.

Applic.:   Submit CV via e-mail stating studies and prior experience and a cover letter stating disposition to work for 4-8 weeks.

Notes: Bring mountain boots and raincoats or waterproofs.

Archaeological Field Methods Field School

Dept of Archaeology, Flinders University of South Australia
GPO Box 2100, Adelaide SA 5001 Australia
Tel.: ++61 (8) 8201 3520 - Fax: ++61 (8) 8201 2784
E-mail: lynley.wallis@flinders.edu.au
*http://ehlt.flinders.edu.au/archaeology/fieldwork/field_schools/f
ield_methods_1/*

Desc.: This fieldschool provides direct experience in a range of archaeological field methods, including general site recording, mapping, survey, site location, assessment, excavation, sorting and artefact analysis. There may be some lecture and/or workshop content, but the school will mainly be directed towards intensive field training in small groups in real-life situations. This fieldschool is being run in partnership with local Nyungar communities, South Coast Natural Resource Management, Applied Archaeology, The National Trust of Australia (WA), WA Dept of Indigenous Affairs and Flinders University in southwest Australia.

Per.: Late Pleistocene and Holocene.

Country: Australia.

Loc.: Various field sites around Esperance in south-west Western Australia.

Travel: Participants will be required to fly to Adelaide at their own cost; then all transport to the field site will be via plane, 4wd and/or bus arranged by the team leader at no additional cost to participants.

Dur.: 14 days; April.

Age: Minimum 18; Maximum 75 or older if fit.

Qualif.: No previous experience necessary.

Work: Survey and recording of archaeological sites, including rock art; photography; offset surveying; total station surveying; excavation of rock shelters and open sites; stone artefact recording.

Lang.: English.

Accom.: Cabins or tents depending on the particular activities being undertaken; when necessary camping equipment can be provided upon prior arrangement with the team leader.

Cost: AUD$3,000 tuition for international participants; AUD$1,750 tuition for Australian participants. Additional field cost contribution TBA.

Applic.: Deadline March 21st; see website or contact Lynley Wallis for details.

Notes: All costs are ex-Adelaide; please note that at the time of printing the field cost contribution had not been determined, however we are hoping to keep it under AUD$500 per participant.

Archaeology at Ben Lomond

The National Trust for Scotland Wemyss House
28 Charlotte Square, Edinburgh Scotland EH2 4ET UK
Tel.: ++44 (131) 243 9470
Fax: ++44 (131) 243 9301
E-mail thistlecamps@nts.org.uk
www.thistlecamps.org.uk

Desc.:	This camp is for those interested in the history of the mountain at the centre of Scotland's first National Park. Survey work has identified over 200 archaeological features on the hill slopes above Rowardennan. Recently the NTS Ranger at Ben Lomond has created a Hidden History Trail at Ardess. Survey plans and small-scale excavation are undertaken in order to find out more about the archaeological features on this trail.
Per.:	18th and 19th centuries.
Country:	United Kingdom.
Loc.:	Slopes of Ben Lomond above Rowardennan (Scotland).
Travel:	Pick-up and drop-off in Edinburgh. Nearest train station in Balloch.
Dur.:	1-2 weeks; July to September.
Age:	Minimum 18.
Qualif.:	No experience necessary. Professional archaeologists supervise and provide instruction in excavation techniques.
Work:	Excavation. Slopes are quite steep and participants must be fit to walk uphill carrying survey equipment and digging tools.
Lang.:	English.
Accom.:	Rowardennan Youth Hostel, provided with showers, lounge, dining room, telephone and drying room.
Cost:	GB£120/week (GB£105 students, unwaged or retired people).
Applic.:	Inquire for details.
Notes:	Bring raingear and warm clothing. See also: Thistle Camps.

Archaeology Field Research Program

Corpus Christi Museum of Science and History, Texas A&M University
1900 N. Chaparral, Corpus Christi, Texas 78401 USA
Tel.: ++1 (361) 826 4662
E-mail: bobd@cctexas.com
www.tamuk.edu/psycsoci/anth/anth.htm;
www.cctexas.com/?fuseaction=main.view&page=

Desc.:	The Field Research Program offers a high-quality educational experience for university students and volunteers. The Lower Nueces River Valley (South Texas) is an area of complex prehistoric hunter/gatherer traditions over 2500 years prior to European contact. Excavations in select habitation sites are yielding information about village tool making, hunting, food preparation, pottery use and related domestic activities, while a field laboratory is set up to process and analyze recovered artefact materials.
Per.:	Archaic and Late Prehistoric (1170 BC to 1770 AD).
Country:	United States.
Loc.:	South Texas.
Travel:	Meeting point at Corpus Christi airport (Texas).
Dur.:	2-7 weeks; June to July.
Age:	Minimum 18.
Qualif.:	No experience necessary.
Work:	Excavation, survey, laboratory work.
Lang.:	English.
Accom.:	Field Headquarters, tent camping with amenities.
Cost:	US$300 per 2-week session. Meals, local transportation and most equipment provided.
Applic.:	Online form on the website www.cctexas.com.
Notes:	See websites for pictures, field reports and additional info.

ArchaeoSpain — The Roman Theatre of Clunia

PO Box 1331
Farmington, Connecticut 06034 USA
Tel./Fax: ++1 (866) 932 0003
E-mail: programs@archaeospain.com
www.archaeospain.com

Desc.: ArchaeoSpain participants join a field crew at the Clunia archaeological excavation alongside archaeologists from the universities of Valladolid, Burgos and Barcelona. The excavation focuses on the city's theatre, the largest of its kind in the Iberian peninsula.

Per.: Roman.

Country: Spain.

Loc.: Burgos province.

Travel: Details provided upon application.

Dur.: 4 weeks; July.

Age: Minimum 18.

Qualif.: No experience necessary.

Work: Excavation, land survey, mapping, photography and conservation of artefacts. Work is physically demanding in the heat. Participants should be in reasonable physical condition and good health.

Lang.: English and Spanish. While ability to speak Spanish is not a prerequisite, participants will be immersed in the language daily, with the hope that their spoken Spanish improves.

Accom.: House.

Cost: US/Canada: US$2,450; UK: GB£1,250. Other countries: EUR1,850. Meals, transportation, excursions and insurance included. Travel expenses not included.

Applic.: Online form.

Notes: Academic credit available with approval from home institution.

Archeodig Project: Researching a Roman Coastal Settlement on Poggio del Molino, Populonia

c/o Carolina Megale
Piazza G. Matteotti 52, Livorno 57126 Italy
Mob.: ++39 (339) 754 4894
E-mail: carolina@archeodig.net   www.archeodig.net

Desc.:	Research on a Roman coastal settlement in Populonia, Tuscany, to answer questions about a period of Populonia and its territory.
Per.:	Roman Period to the Middle Ages.
Country:	Italy.
Loc.:	Poggio del Molino, Piombino (Livorno), between the Ligurian Sea and the Tyrrhenian Sea.
Travel:	Florence or Pisa airport; train to Campiglia Marittima (Piombino).
Dur.:	Minimum 1 week. Summer term: May to June (6 weeks). Autumn term: September to October (6 weeks).
Age:	Minimum 16.
Qualif.:	No prerequisites or archaeological experience required.
Work:	Introduction to archaeological theory; excavation practice with professional archaeologists; documentation; excavation and drawing of late-antique tombs; technical relief and structural analysis of walls, paintings, mosaics; cataloguing mobile artefacts; collecting organic samples; preliminary restoration.
Lang.:	Italian and English.
Accom.:	Single, double or multiple rooms in furnished lodgings with basic comforts (light, gas, bed, mattress, toilet), a few kms offsite.
Cost:	EUR500 per week, tuition included; room, board and transport to/from the site EUR250-450.
Applic.:	Inquire for details.
Notes:	Academic credit through Tuscany Archaeological Bureau. Bring a 4-in steel pointing trowel, durable yet cool clothing, reinforced safety shoes, sunhat, raincoat, gardening gloves, sunscreen.

Archeostage — Olloy-Sur-Viroin Archeological Dig

Les Forges St Roch and le Centre de Recherches Archéologiques de l'Université Libre de Bruxelles

Asbl, 7 Ch. Du Try Châlons, 5660 Couvin Belgium

Tel.: ++32 (60) 312 236 /(60) 347 423

E-mail: archeostage@skynet.be   www.archeostage.com

Desc.:	The excavation is centred on a protohistoric fortification of the "Tène" period, accompanied by a necropolis that is comprised of several tens of stone "marchets" or hillocks. The fortress is located on a rock headland that rises approximately 230ft (70m) from the Viroin River extends over 2,5ha with its double rampart is still visible by several meters in height. It is an exceptional archaeological site owing to its state of conservation and the chronological elements that it can deliver.
Per.:	Second Age of Iron or "Gallic" period.
Country:	Belgium.
Loc.:	"Olloy-sur-Viroin", country of Viroinval (southern Belgium).
Travel:	Details provided upon application.
Dur.:	9-28 days; July.
Age:	Minimum 17.
Qualif.:	No previous experience necessary.
Work:	Audio-visual excavations, talks and conferences, films, information retrievals, treatment of the discovered material, stroll guided prospect techniques, data-recording and processing techniques (Stratigraphic Units), drawing, topography.
Lang.:	English, French.
Accom.:	Camping on site.
Cost:	EUR290/9 days, EUR560/18 days, EUR820/27 days. Meals, workshops, visits, lectures and insurances included.
Applic.:	Online form.

ArcheoVenezia Archaeological Field Work Camp

ArcheoClub d'Italia
Cannaregio, 1376/a, 30121 Venice Italy
Tel./Fax: ++39 (041) 710 515
E-mail: info@archeove.com
www.archeove.com; www.lazzarettonuovo.com

Desc.:	ArcheoVenezia is the Venetian division of Archeoclub d'Italia, a non-profit association dedicated to conservation of cultural heritage. In 1987, it began a project in the Venetian lagoon for the recovery of the island of Lazzaretto Novo, once (1468-1792) used for the prevention of spreading plague (here was coined the word "quarantine" from the preventive isolation of suspected vessels, goods and passengers). Trial excavations are carried out on the island in various areas, included the priorado, to verify the wall structures and the foundations present on the island as part of an archaeological project on the history of public health.
Per.:	15th to 18th centuries and precedent periods.
Country:	Italy.
Loc.:	Island of Lazzaretto Nuovo (Venice Lagoon), Venice.
Travel:	Train to Venice, then vaporetto (public boat) to the island.
Dur.:	7-10 days; June to September.
Age:	Minimum 18.
Qualif.:	No experience necessary.
Work:	Onsite training covers the correct use of instruments and tools, identification and retrieval of stratigraphic units (SU), examination and classification of finds, archaeological drawing, survey, graphical reconstruction.
Lang.:	Italian, French, English.
Accom.:	Lodging with hot water. Meals prepared by a cook with volunteers.
Cost:	EUR400, plus approximately EUR30 for Venice boat pass.
Applic.:	Deadline 1 month before the beginning of the workcamp.

ASEPAM

Centre du Patrimoine Minier
4, rue Weisgerber
68 160 Sainte-Marie-Aux-Mines France
Tel.: ++33 (03) 8958 6211 - Fax: ++33 (03) 8958 6897
E-mail: chantier@asepam.org
www.asepam.org

Desc.: The galleries of these ancient silver mines are not as large as modern ones. Since the 10th century, miners dug miles of galleries through the heavy hard rock at a rate of about 4in/day (10 cm/day). The ASEPAM proposes to discover this universe and live the new "adventure of the mines" by participating on this revival.

Per.: 18th and 19th centuries.

Country: France.

Loc.: Sainte Marie-aux-Mines, Haut-Rhin, Alsace.

Travel: Details provided upon application.

Dur.: Minimum 1 week; maximum 3 weeks; July.

Age: Minimum 18.

Qualif.: No experience necessary. Professional archaeologists supervise and provide instruction in excavation techniques.

Work: Fine excavation, geophysical prospecting surveys, photographic and video recording.

Lang.: English, French, German.

Accom.: Large house in the mountains, the Zillardthof.

Cost: EUR60/week or EUR90 for 3 weeks.

Applic.: Inquire for details.

Notes: Online form.

Augusta Trajana–Beroe–Borui Rescue Excavations Project

Balkan Heritage (BH) Field School
204 Sveta Troica str., BG-6004 Stara Zagora Bulgaria
Tel.: ++359 (42) 235 402 /888 165 402
E-mail: balkanheritage@gmail.com
www.bhfieldschool.org

Desc.:	Stara Zagora Regional History Museum has implemented an intensive programme of rescue excavations of the ancient town Augusta Trajana-Beroe-Borui, where mainly Roman and Late Antique layers are to be studied.
Per.:	Roman (107-370 AD), Late Antique (370-590 AD).
Country:	Bulgaria.
Loc.:	Stara Zagora (south-central region).
Travel:	Transfer from the nearest airports of Sofia and Burgas is available. Otherwise, participants may travel by train or bus.
Dur.:	2 to 8 weeks; June to August.
Age:	Minimum 16.
Qualif.:	No experience necessary.
Work:	Excavation, survey, laboratory work, lectures, workshops. All participants will receive BH field school certificate specifying fieldwork hours, educational modules and visited sightseeing. Up to 4 field school sessions per year are available, including 3 modules: fieldwork, educational course and excursions.
Lang.:	English
Accom.:	Hotel accommodation with showers, air-conditioning and TV.
Cost:	About EUR899/2 weeks (-15% for each subsequent session). Tuition, fieldwork activities, room & board, excursion expenses, medical insurance and administrative costs are included.
Applic.:	Online form on www.bhfieldschool.org.
Notes:	7% of admission fee supports heritage protection fund activities.

AVSO — Association of Voluntary Service Organisations

Rue Henri Stacquet 61
1030 Bruxelles Belgium
Tel.:++32 (2) 230 6813 - Fax:++32 (2) 245 6297
E-mail: info@avso.org
www.avso.org

Desc.:   AVSO forms a European platform for national and international non-profit organisations active in the field of longer term voluntary service. They lobby for the legal status of volunteers and enhanced mobility within Europe and aim to broaden participation in voluntary service among new organisations in the non-profit sector and among individuals who may traditionally not have access to volunteer opportunities (disabled, socially/ economically disadvantaged and ethnic minorities).

Country: Worldwide.

Dur.:   6-18 months, varies with organisation.

Age: 18-25 (13-30 for the "Youth in Action Programme").

Qualif.:   No experience necessary.

Work: Heritage conservation, community development, culture, education, environment, human rights, various.

Lang.:   Language and intercultural training provided.

Accom.:   Room & board, small stipend, insurance and other benefits in accordance with volunteer status.

Cost: EUR500 registration fee plus US$10/day; room & board and transfers included. Personal expenses, travel and airport tax not included.

Applic.:   Contact project organisation. Residents of the European Union or an applicant country only. AVSO does not itself organise volunteer exchange programmes, applicants should contact directly the AVSO members listed in the website.

Baga Gazaryn Chuluu Excavation

Center for the Study of Eurasian Nomads
2158 Palomar Ave.
Ventura, California 93001 USA
Tel./Fax: ++1 (805) 653 2607
E-mail: jkimball@csen.org
www.csen.org

Desc.: American and Mongolian archaeologists have initiated excavations at Baga Gazaryn Chuluu in the desert-steppe zone of Middle Gobi province in Mongolia. Ancient petroglyphs can be discovered on the granite outcrops. Stone stelae, erected by early Turkic nomads, are located in the main valley running between the towering peaks. Volunteers assist archaeologists from US and Mongolian research institutions in beginning the survey and in conducting several small-scale excavations of Bronze and Early Iron Age (800-400 BC) burial and habitation sites.

Per.: Upper Palaeolithic to 20th century AD: Neolithic, Bronze Age, Early Iron Age, Medieval.

Country: Mongolia.

Loc.: South-central Mongolia, Middle Gobi province, approximately 30mi (50km) north of the city of Mandalgov.

Travel: Meeting point arranged with application.

Dur.: 3 or 6 weeks; July to August.

Age: Minimum 20.

Qualif.: No experience required. Training provided.

Work: Bioarchaeological excavations and artefact processing. Cultural excursions, jeep trips into the true sand Gobi of Mongolia to collect ore samples and visit Mongolian archaeological research sites.

Lang.: English.

Accom.: Camping (no electricity). Bring a tent, sleeping bag and mat.

Cost: 3-week session US$1,200 (students), US$1,400 (non-students).

Expenses at the site, 12 nights of lodging in expedition rental in Ulaanbaatar and bus/van transport to/from the site included. Airfare, insurance and expenses in Ulaanbaatar not included.

Applic.: Online form at http://csen.org. Mail application and deposit of US$300 by April 15th, final payment by June 10th. Deadlines are strict to allow time for visa processing. A visa will not be granted until the entire contribution is paid. The organization will facilitate obtaining visas for all participants.

Notes: Challenging field conditions, moderate workload (notably hiking), living in tents under semi-desert conditions and a meat-based diet. Consult the website for clothing and equipment recommendations. See also: Center for the Study of Eurasian Nomads.

Balkan Heritage Field School

204 Sveta Troica str.
6004 Stara Zagora Bulgaria
Tel.: ++359 (42) 235 402 /888 165 402
E-mail: balkanheritage@gmail.com
www.bhfieldschool.org

Desc.:	Balkan Heritage (est. 2003) functions as a legal part of Balkan Heritage Foundation, Bulgaria, and implements volunteer workcamps and study projects focused on protection, restoration and promotion of sites, artefacts and practices presenting the cultural heritage of south-eastern Europe with participation of students, scholars and volunteers from all over the world.
Per.:	Various.
Country:	Bulgaria, Macedonia and other countries in south-eastern Europe.
Loc.:	Various sites in south-eastern Europe.
Travel:	Volunteers are responsible for travel to the project site.
Dur.:	Varies with project (refer to the website for details).
Age:	Minimum 16.
Qualif.:	Varies with project (refer to the website for details).
Work:	Field-school sessions combine 3 basic modules: educational (lectures, trainings and workshops), practical (excavations, lab work, fieldtrips, documentation, restoration and conservation, etc.) and excursions to archaeological and cultural sites near the project location.
Lang.:	English.
Accom.:	Varies with project (refer to the website for details).
Cost:	Varies with project (refer to the website for details). Typically, project fees are all inclusive.
Applic.:	Online form.
Notes:	All BH participants receive academic credit worthy certificates.

Bamburgh Research Project
Bamburgh Castle
Bamburgh, Northumberland NE UK
Tel.: ++44 (1904) 330 727
E-mail: paulgething@bamburghresearchproject.co.uk
www.bamburghresearchproject.co.uk

Desc.:   The project is centred on the Bamburgh Castle and is dedicated to using the most modern field techniques, implemented by experienced field archaeologists, to provide training for both students and volunteers. There are sites under excavation both within the castle and in the castle environs. In addition, survey projects are undertaken with a fully functioning media department dedicated to filming the archaeological process.

Per.:   Multi-period; early Medieval to modern.

Country: United Kingdom.

Loc.:   Bamburgh Castle, 50mi (80km) north of Newcastle on the north-east coast.

Travel: Nearest railway station is Berwick on Tweed, 15mi (24km) from Bamburgh on the main east coastline. Regular bus service from Berwick to Bamburgh.

Dur.:   Mid June to end of August.

Age: All ages.

Qualif.:   No experience necessary. Youth and physically disabled volunteers are welcome, please contact for arrangements.

Work: Excavation, training, field walking and test pitting.

Lang.:   English.

Accom.:   Fully equipped campsite. Bring own tent and personal items.

Cost: GB£95/week. Tuition, travel to and from the site daily, food and camp space included.

Applic.:   Limited placements available.

Bektashi Tekke of Melan, Albania

Albanian National Trust
Butrinti Str, Saranda Albania
Tel.: ++355 (682) 058 244 /++1 (773) 373 3109 (USA)
E-mail: visitbutrint@albmail.com; klj@uchicago.edu
www.butrinti.com

Desc.:	The site chosen for the excavation is rich with remains of many early cultures, including Illyrian, Roman and Byzantine. This valley was also controlled by the Ottoman Empire, which brought many changes, including the introduction of Islam. The project focuses on a Roman-period mosaic floor, some yet undated burials and a Byzantine building, as well as opening other areas to further explore the Islamic heritage of the site.
Per.:	Roman, Byzantine, Ottoman.
Country:	Albania.
Loc.:	Drinos Valley, near the city of Gjirokaster (southern Albania).
Travel:	Details provided upon application.
Dur.:	4-8 weeks; July to September.
Age:	Minimum 18.
Qualif.:	No experience necessary.
Work:	Excavation, survey, laboratory work.
Lang.:	English.
Accom.:	The team will be staying and eating at the Bektashi tekke, a functioning monastery..
Cost:	Room & board US$25/day. Travel and other personal expenses not included.
Applic.:	Contact Katie Johnson (klj@uchicago.edu) or Auron Tare (visitbutrint@albmail.com).
Notes:	This excavation is groundbreaking in its international cooperation and examination of the effects of several cultural periods upon modern Albania.

Belize Valley Archaeology Reconnaissance Project

Belize Institute of Archaeology
c/o National Institute of Culture and History
Museum Building, Culvert road, Belmopan City Belize
Tel.: ++(501) 822 302 /822 3307
E-mail: archaeology@bvar.org   www.bvar.org

Desc.:	BVAR's operations on the site of Baking Pot involve students in all aspects of the archaeological investigations, from the setting of excavation units to the production of site maps, including daily lab work where students participate in the processing and documentation of the artefacts recovered from the site (a wide range of ceramic and lithic artefacts and human and animal remains). Weekly lectures present an overview of Mayan civilisation and provide introduction to other specific topics (ceramic analysis, archaeological survey methods, human osteology, ancient Maya ritual, ideology, hieroglyphic writing).
Per.:	Pre-classic through post-classic Maya.
Country:	Belize.
Loc.:	San Ignacio, Cayo District, 72mi (116km) west of Belize City.
Travel:	Pick-up at Belize International airport (BZE).
Dur.:	2-8 weeks; June to July.
Age:	Minimum 18.
Qualif.:	Good health for high physical, emotional and mental demands.
Work:	Full training in survey, reconnaissance, excavation, analysis, GPS.
Lang.:	English, Spanish useful.
Accom.:	Modest, with meals consisting of local fare.
Cost:	US$1,950/month; field school US$975/2 weeks. Lodging, weekday meals and transportation to and from the site included. Travel and incidental expenses not included.
Applic.:	Online form on: http://bvar.org/application.htm.
Notes:	Academic credit through Galen Univ./Univ. of Indianapolis.

71

Bitola Heritage Workcamp

Balkan Heritage (BH) Field School
204 Sveta Troica str.
BG-6004 Stara Zagora Bulgaria
Tel.: ++359 (42) 235 402 /888 165 402
E-mail: balkanheritage@gmail.com
www.bhfieldschool.org

Desc.:	The workcamp is an archaeological site at Heraclea Lyncestis, an important economic and administrative centre from 4thcentury BC to 6thcentury AD. Volunteers will support the ongoing excavations and the maintenance of the site sectors opened to visitors. They will also be involved in the development of advocacy campaign "Visit the Museum", aiming to raise public awareness towards cultural heritage promotion.
Per.:	Hellenistic, Roman, Late Antique (4th century BC to 6th century AD).
Country:	Macedonia.
Loc.:	Bitola (south-western region).
Travel:	Transfer from the nearest airports of Skopje and Thessaloniki is available. Otherwise, participants may travel by train or bus.
Dur.:	2 weeks; July to August.
Age:	Minimum 16.
Qualif.:	No experience necessary.
Work:	Excavation (digging, brushing, measuring, washing and cataloguing artefacts), survey, maintenance of archaeological sites (painting, removing grass and plants, cutting trees, cleaning and conservation), campaigning.
Lang.:	English.
Accom.:	Hotel accommodation with showers, air-conditioning and TV.
Cost:	About EUR399/2 weeks (-15% for each subsequent BH project). Room & board, excursions/sightseeing tours/entrance fees, workshops, medical insurance and administrative costs included.
Applic.:	Online form on www.bhfieldschool.org.

Brašov Project

Projects Abroad
Aldsworth Parade, Goring
Sussex BN12 4TX UK
Tel.: ++44 (1903) 708 300 - Fax: ++44 (1903) 501 026
E-mail: info@projects-abroad.co.uk
www.projects-abroad.co.uk

Desc.:   Projects Abroad is a global volunteering organisation that sends volunteers to take part in a variety of projects. Its archaeology programme in Romania is based around the historic town of Brašov in Transylvania, considered to be an area of huge archaeological importance. Artefacts dating to BC 4000 have been found as well as Greek, Roman and Dacic remains.

Per.:   Various.

Country: Romania.

Loc.:   Alba Iulia and Brašov.

Travel: Projects Abroad can arrange travel for volunteers if they wish. Volunteers are met at the airport by a member of staff.

Dur.:   Minimum 1 month; May to October.

Age: Minimum 17.

Qualif.:   No experience necessary.

Work: Excavation, historic structure restoration, writing interpretive brochures. Full training provided.

Lang.:   English.

Accom.:   In local hostels, with local families or on site. Food is provided by staff or local host families/supervisors.

Cost: Project costs range from GB£1,295.

Applic.:   Online or by telephone.

Notes: Volunteers will receive details before departure of any equipment and kit they may need to bring.

Build Your Own PIT Project

Passport In Time Clearinghouse
PO Box 15728, Rio Rancho, NM 87174-5728 USA
Tel./Fax: ++1 (800) 281 9176 /(505) 896 1136
E-mail: volunteer@passportintime.com
www.passportintime.com

Desc.:	This organisation gives experienced volunteers the opportunity to develop a volunteer project on the Malheur National Forest in Oregon. There is an "artist in residence" programme for volunteers, but this site is also a great base from which to explore the natural and cultural history of eastern Oregon.
Per.:	Archaic through historic periods.
Country:	United States.
Loc.:	Malheur National Forest, John Day, Oregon.
Travel:	Flight to Boise Idaho or Portland Oregon, drive by auto 4-5 hours to John Day. No public transportation.
Dur.:	Minimum 10 hours/week, 5 days or more; year round.
Age:	Minimum 18.
Qualif.:	No previous experience necessary. The requisites are skill, motivation, ability to work with little supervision.
Work:	Possible projects include scanning historic photographs, computer database entry, writing an article on local history, landscaping at historic buildings or monitoring archaeological and historic sites (site monitoring in summer only).
Lang.:	English.
Accom.:	Historic forest supervisor's home with kitchen, bath and laundry.
Cost:	No cost. Meals and personal expenses not included.
Applic.:	Registration is open year round. See website for details.

Bunifat Project

Drepanon Archaeological Group - Gruppi Archeologici d'Italia
C.da Cutusio, 527 a/bis
91025 Marsala (TP) Italy
Tel./Fax: ++39 (339) 243 3729
E-mail: antonfilippi@libero.it
www.drepanon.org

Desc.:	Drepanon Archaeological Group is the division of Gruppi Archeologici d'Italia for the northern area of Trapani province. Since 2007, Bunifat Project is organised in the Natural Reserve area of Monte Bonifato (Alcamo-TP), a site of great archaeological and environmental interest where several remains of an archaic-Medieval site rest. The project has scientific and didactic purposes, involving volunteers and high school and undergraduate students of the surrounding territory. An excavation has been conducted, in cooperation with the local Fine Arts Bureau, as well as a topographic survey of all the surfacing buildings in the area.
Per.:	8th to 5th centuries BC; 11th to 14th centuries AD.
Country:	Italy.
Loc.:	R.N.O. Monte Bonifato, Alcamo, western Sicily.
Travel:	Train or plane to Palermo, then bus to Alcamo.
Dur.:	2 sessions of 7 days; July to August.
Age:	Minimum 18.
Qualif.:	No previous experience necessary.
Work:	Archaeological reconnaissance, topographic survey, stratigraphic excavation, collection of findings, drawing, etc.
Lang.:	English and Italian.
Accom.:	Housing with showers and facilities. Meals prepared with volunteers' help.
Cost:	EUR350/week.
Applic.:	Deadline for application June 15th.

Butser Ancient Farm

Nexus House, Gravel Hill, Waterlooville Hampshire PO8 0QE UK
Chalton Lane, Chalton, Waterlooville, Hampshire PO8 0BG
Tel.: ++44 (7980) 563 872 /(23) 9259 8838
Fax: ++44 (23) 9259 8838
www.butser.org.uk

Desc.: This is a replica farm of what would have existed in the British Iron Age. Founded in 1972, it moved to its present site at Bascomb Copse in 1992. The farm has buildings, structures, animals, and crops of the kind that existed at that time. The museum functions as an open-air laboratory where research into the Iron Age and Roman periods goes on using the methods and materials that were available at that time and by applying modern science to ancient problems.

Per.: British Iron Age to Roman; 300 BC to 400 AD.

Country: United Kingdom.

Loc.: Petersfield.

Travel: Details provided upon application.

Dur.: 2-3 days minimum; May to October.

Age: Minimum 18.

Qualif.: No experience necessary.

Work: Various tasks. Practical workshops include gathering herbs for simple medicinal recipes, and metalworking.

Lang.: English.

Accom.: No room or board provided.

Cost: No fees charged to volunteer. Practical workshops cost between GB£20-100 per day.

Applic.: Telephone the office at ++44 (23) 9259 8838.

Caer Alyn Archaeological and Heritage Project

Lliy Nr Wrexham,
North East Wales UK
Tel.: ++44 (1244) 321858 /(7947) 768446
E-mail: fillcox@yahoo.co.uk; alan.brown@stfc.ac.uk
www.caeralyn.org

Desc.:	The Caer Alyn Archaeological & Heritage Project has a team made up of both professionals and volunteers, with the main aim to survey and protect the Caer Alyn promontory fort, near the village of Llay in Denbighshire and fully investigate the landscape that surrounds it.
Per.:	Late Bronze Age to post Medieval.
Country:	Wales, United Kingdom.
Loc.:	Lliy Nr Wrexham, north-east Wales.
Travel:	Train to Wrexham or Chester, then bus to Lliy.
Dur.:	1 day for volunteers. See website for training digs.
Age:	Minimum 16; maximum 75, or older if fit; 8-16 for youth programme.
Qualif.:	No previous experience necessary.
Work:	Training; geophysical survey, excavation techniques, surveying, recording, photography; 10.00-14.00, Saturdays.
Lang.:	English.
Accom.:	Camping or local guest house.
Cost:	GB£100 /week tuition for training digs, or GB£40/year if volunteering for Saturdays only.
Applic.:	See website.

Canterbury Archaeological Trust Ltd.

Whitefriars Office
c/o 92a Broad Street, Canterbury, Kent CT1 2LU UK
Tel.: ++44 (1227) 765 364 /462 062
Fax: ++44 (1227) 784 724
E-mail: cat.whitefriars@virgin.net; admin@canterburytrust.co.uk
www.canterburytrust.co.uk

Desc.: Canterbury Archaeological Trust (CAT) was established in 1976 and is engaged in a series of major excavations at "Whitefriars" in the heart of the historic city of Canterbury. Archaeologists expect to find multi-period evidence and more of the Whitefriars friary.

Per.: Late Iron Age, Roman, Anglo-Saxon, Norman, Medieval and post-Medieval to modern.

Country: United Kingdom.

Loc.: Canterbury, Kent, south-east England.

Travel: Train, bus connections from the port of Dover, 14mi (23km) away and London, 56mi (90km) away. Canterbury has 2 rail stations: the site is a 5-min walk from Canterbury East rail station and directly opposite the bus station and a 15-min walk from Canterbury West rail station.

Dur.: July to January.

Age: Minimum 16.

Qualif.: No experience is necessary. Basic training provided.

Work: Excavation and site recording depending upon volunteer ability. Washing finds as appropriate.

Lang.: English.

Accom.: Either youth hostel in town or campsite 3mi out of town.

Cost: No project fee. Room & board not included.

Applic.: Write or e-mail Whitefriars site directors, A.Hicks and M.Houliston.

Notes: Bring weather-appropriate clothing, steel-toed boots and personal trowel (or buy a trowel at the project).

Capena Excavation Project

School of Languages & Literatures, University of Cape Town
Dr Roman Roth, Private Bag, Rondebosch, 7700 South Africa
Tel.: ++27 (21) 650 2611
E-mail: roman.roth@uct.ac.za
www.classics.uct.ac.za/?page=archaeology

Desc.:	Excavation of a central Italian town situated in the Tiber Valley, a uniquely long and undisturbed sequence from early Etruscan to Late Roman times. The town was historically important as an ally of Rome and involved in the food supply of the metropolis. Its affluence is documented by wealthy tombs.
Per.:	Early Etruscan to Late Roman.
Country:	Italy.
Loc.:	La Civitucola, Capena, provincia di Roma.
Travel:	Flight to Rome (ROM/FCO), train/bus 22mi (35km) north to Capena.
Dur.:	4 weeks; July.
Age:	Minimum 18; maximum 70, or older if fit.
Qualif.:	No previous experience necessary.
Work:	On-site training on use of instruments and tools, identification and retrieval of stratigraphic units (SU), examination and classification of finds (pottery, building materials, metals, glass fragments), archaeological drawing, survey (total station) and graphical reconstruction. Excursions to regional archaeological sites on weekends.
Lang.:	English, German, Italian.
Accom.:	Shared rooms in a renaissance monastery complex (see www.casacapena.com) in Capena (about 2mi/3km from site).
Cost:	Approximately US$800/EUR650/week; room & board (breakfast and lunch at the house, dinner at a local restaurant) included.
Applic.:	Registration deadline April 15th. Contact the director by e-mail.

Carnuntum

Archaeologischer Park Carnuntum
Hauptstrasse 1, A-2404 Petronell-Carnuntum Austria
Tel.: ++43 (0) 2163 2882
Fax: ++43 (0) 2163 2884
E-mail: franz.humer@noel.gv.at
www.carnuntum.co.at

Desc.:	Carnuntum is the largest archaeological site in Austria. After centuries of demolition the former capital of the Roman province, Pannonia Superior, is now being systematically excavated. The objectives are to study, rescue and present this site in a sensitively restored manner using modern monument preservation techniques while at the same time making sensible economic use of this resource. The excavations of a part of the civilian town in Petronell are combined with reconstruction, scientific publications and inclusion of the visitors to the archaeological fieldwork.
Per.:	Roman, 1st to 5th centuries AD.
Country:	Austria.
Loc.:	Villages of Petronell-Carnuntum and Bad Deutsch-Altenburg, Province of Lower Austria, 25mi (40km) east of Vienna.
Travel:	Train or bus.
Dur.:	6 weeks.
Age:	Minimum 18.
Qualif.:	Satisfactory academic grade and interest in archaeology and history.
Work:	Excavation, documentation, mapping, etc.
Lang.:	German, English.
Accom.:	None provided. Various accommodations available in the villages.
Cost:	No project fee. Room & board and insurance not included.
Applic.:	By ordinary mail, fax or e-mail.
Notes:	Bring work clothes and gloves.

Castanheiro do Vento

Av. Prof. Guilherme Cunha
Freixo de Numão
5155-235 F Portugal
Tel.: ++351 (279) 589 573
E-mail: ana.m.vale@gmail.com

Desc.: The research project based on the excavations of Castanheiro do Vento started in 1998. Every summer, archaeological diggings are made on the top of a hill, which allowed the identification of 3 concentric walls intercepted by the so called "bastions" (semi-circular structures) and several entrances. This kind of sites is usually interpreted in the Iberian Peninsula as fortified settlements. However the research undertaken has been questioning this approach. It is thought that Castanheiro do Vento was not built due to conflicts during the 3rd millennium BC, but it enables other connexions, such as monument, memory, performance, landscape, territory, place and image.

Per.: 3rd millennium BC.

Country: Portugal.

Loc.: Horta do Douro, VN de Foz Côa, Guarda, Portugal.

Travel: Flight to Oporto, then by train to Freixo de Numão.

Dur.: 3-4 weeks; July. Inquire for long term opportunities.

Age: Minimum 18.

Qualif.: Archaeological experience welcome.

Work: Fieldwork (digging, drawing, photography, topography) and museum activities (washing and cataloguing materials). Seminars related to the research given by the directors.

Lang.: Portuguese, English, Spanish, French.

Accom.: In shared bedrooms (sleeping bags required).

Cost: Funding may be available for accommodation costs.

Applic.: E-mail CV before the end of May.

Castell Henllys Training Excavation

School of Archaeology, Classics and Egyptology
Univ. of Liverpool, Centre for Manx Studies
6 Kingswood Grove, Douglas, Isle of Man IM1 3LX UK
Tel.: ++44 (1624) 695 150 - Fax: ++44 (1624) 678 752
E-mail: cms@liv.ac.uk
www.liv.ac.uk/sace/research/projects/castell-henllys/index.htm

Desc.:	This project is investigating an Iron Age inland promontory fort and nearby Iron Age and Romano-British farmsteads, some with evidence of post-Roman activity. Much of the fort has been examined and experimental buildings have been constructed on their original locations, but survey and excavation continues on other nearby Iron Age and Romano-British settlements to understand the whole landscape and its development.
Per.:	Iron Age and Roman.
Country:	United Kingdom.
Loc.:	Fishguard, 8mi (12km) from the site.
Travel:	Details provided upon application.
Dur.:	Minimum 2 weeks; July to August.
Age:	Minimum 16.
Qualif.:	No experience necessary.
Work:	Excavation.
Lang.:	English.
Accom.:	Tent camping with toilets and showers. Tents available to rent if required. Students help with campsite duties on a rotation basis.
Cost:	GB£170/week for initial 2 weeks; GB£120/week for each subsequent week. Tuition, campsite and food included. Field-school credit available, GB£2,150 for 6 weeks including 2-week survey in Ireland.
Applic.:	Contact Dr. Harold Mytum, Director.

CCIVS — Coordinating Committee for International Volunteers

1 rue Miollis, 75015 Paris France
Tel.: ++33 (1) 4568 4936
Fax: ++33 (1) 4273 0521
E-mail: ccivs@unesco.org
www.unesco.org/ccivs/

Desc.:	This international non-governmental organisation plays a coordinating role in the sphere of voluntary service. Historical monuments and archaeological sites have been maintained, restored and preserved by volunteers. The actions and projects concerning cultural heritage preservation involve non-qualified persons and young people, from any background. These activities, led by professionals, also aim at initiating, training and developing restoration techniques. CCIVS organises, in co-operation with the cultural division of UNESCO, numerous workcamps for the preservation of cultural heritage.
Per.:	Modern/contemporary.
Country:	Over 100 countries.
Loc.:	Various.
Travel:	Details provided with specific project.
Dur.:	Typically 3-4 weeks but longer terms are available; year round.
Age:	Inquire for programmes for volunteers under 18.
Qualif.:	No experience necessary for workcamps.
Work:	Projects may involve landscaping, reconstruction and restoration of buildings, etc., in a workcamp situation.
Lang.:	Local language of the member organisation.
Accom.:	Ranges from tent camping to hostels to hotels.
Cost:	Varies with each member organisation.
Applic.:	Contact member organisation directly. See website for links.
Notes:	CCIVS produces several publications on volunteer service. Contact them for list of and orders. See also: UNESCO.

Chateau Ganne

Université de Caen
Centre de recherches archéologiques et historiques médiévales
14032 Caen Cedex France
Tel. ++33 (02) 3156 5919 - Fax ++33 (02) 3156 5495
E-mail: amflambard@unicaen.fr
http://pagesperso-orange.fr/amfl/ganne/chantier.html

Desc.:	This impressive fortification, unique to Normandy, includes 2 main enclosures connected by an old tower. Close to the castles of Exeter and Berri-Pomeroy, the fort was built by the family of Pommeraye, which took part in the conquest of England alongside William of Orange and received in compensation important possessions in Sommerset. The multidisciplinary study consists of taking a precise survey of the fortification and the position of the stones, allowing for their consolidation, excavation and stratigraphic survey.
Per.:	Medieval; 11th and 12th centuries.
Country:	France.
Loc.:	Normandy, 22mi (35km) south of Caen.
Travel:	Train to Caen, Green Bus of Calvados to Clécy (line Caen-Flers).
Dur.:	6 days/week; 2-3 weeks; July.
Age:	Minimum 18
Qualif.:	No previous experience necessary.
Work:	Scouring and excavation, archaeological drawing, cleaning and classification of materials, data-processing and recording. Monday to Saturday..
Lang.:	French.
Accom.:	Basic hotel ("gîte d'étape"). Bring sleeping bag, towel and flashlight/torch.
Cost:	EUR10 application. Room & board included.
Applic.:	Online form in French.

Cirò Archaeological Field Work Camp

Ionic Archaeological Group "L. Magrin"
CIRA – International Center for Archaeological Research
Via XXV Aprile 16, 88060 Montepaone Lido (Cz) Italy
Mob.: ++39 (348) 584 8763 - Fax: ++39 (0967) 576 075
E-mail: toni.re@libero.it
www.antiquariumcropani.it

Desc.: Ionic Archaeological Group is the Calabrese division of CIRA, a non-profit association for research, conservation and development of cultural heritage. In the past years the excavations have been carried out in locations that revealed Prehistoric, Greek, Italic, Roman and Medieval settlements. The "Apollo" project will lead to the excavation and development of a sacred area in the Cirò Marina Commune (the ancient Krimisa) where lies the Greek temple consecrated to Apollo Aleo, dated back to the Archaic to Hellenistic Ages.

Per.: 7th to 4th centuries BC.

Country: Italy.

Loc.: Cirò Marina, Crotone, Calabria.

Travel: Flight to Lamezia Terme or Crotone, train to Crotone or Cirò Marina.

Dur.: Sessions of 15 days; July to August.

Age: Minimum 16.

Qualif.: No previous experience necessary.

Work: Lectures on Calabrese history, training on use of instruments and tools, identification of the Stratigraphic Units (SU), examination and classification of finds, archaeological drawing and survey.

Lang.: English, French and Italian.

Accom.: Local school with showers and shared bathroom. Meals prepared by a cook with volunteers' help.

Cost: EUR300.

Applic.: Deadline for application June 30th.

Club du Vieux Manoir

Ancienne Abbaye du Moncel
60700 Pontpoint France
Tel.: ++33 (3) 4472 3398
Fax: ++33 (3) 4470 1314
E-mail: clubduvieuxmanoir@free.fr
http://cvmclubduvieuxmanoir.free.fr

Desc.: The organisation aims to develop cultural and leisure activities to protect, restore, promote and revitalise the architectural heritage and its relationship with the current cultural and social life. Its goals are to protect and renovate historical monuments and threatened sites; open the restored monuments to the public; create and manage museums; publish historical, archaeological and cultural tourism studies. Works are mostly on castles, villas and forts.

Per: Middle Ages to modern.

Country: France.

Loc.: The regions of Hautes Alpes, Aisne, Oise and Indre.

Travel: See website for details on each project.

Dur.: Usually 15 days in summer; variable terms on non-summer and permanent sites or activities.

Age: Minimum 14-18, varies with project.

Qualif.: No experience necessary. Motivation to protect cultural heritage.

Work: Masonry, general restoration work, archaeological excavations, cleaning/maintaining vegetation, mapping, public education, tourist promotion, cultural interpretation.

Lang.: French.

Accom.: Tent camping.

Cost: EUR14/day, room & board included; EUR15/year membership fee.

Applic.: Online form.

Notes: The organisation runs year round activities, such as guided weekend visits to monuments, painting courses, etc.

Compagnons Batisseurs

Association Nationale Compagnons Bàtisseurs
216, route de Lorient, BP 42037
35920 Rennes Cedex France
Tel.: ++33 (2) 9902 6090 - Fax: ++33 (2) 9902 6070
E-mail: cbvolontariat@compagnonsbatisseurs.org
www.compagnonsbatisseurs.org

Desc.:	This non-profit organisation was born 50 years ago aimed at helping a population hard hit by the damage of World War II. It has been putting solidarity into practice by means of workcamps in reconstruction and restoration as well as promoting peace and better understanding between people from around the world.
Per.:	Various.
Country:	France.
Loc.:	Mainly in the regions of Bretagne, Centre, Midi Pyrénées, Provence Alpes, Côtes d'Azur and abroad throughout Europe.
Travel:	Details provided upon application to specific project.
Dur.:	Varies with project; summer.
Age:	Minimum 18; workcamps for 16-17 years old available.
Qualif.:	No experience necessary.
Work:	Workcamps in masonry, brickwork, painting, carpentry or other skills applied to restoration and reconstruction.
Lang.:	French or language of host country.
Accom.:	Typically group camping.
Cost:	Enquire for details, varies with project duration.
Applic.:	Online form.

Concordia

19 North Street, Portslade
Brighton BN41 1DH UK
Tel.: ++44 (1273) 422 218
Fax: ++44 (1273) 421 182
E-mail: info@concordia-iye.org.uk
www.concordia-iye.org.uk

Desc.: Most Concordia volunteer projects are environmental or renovation projects as well as play schemes or other social projects. There are also long-term opportunities through the European Voluntary Service and other programmes.

Per.: Various.

Country: Over 60 countries worldwide.

Loc.: Most of the time, camps are in small isolated villages and there is not necessarily a car available at the camp.

Travel: Specific details provided for each volunteer project.

Dur.: 2-4 weeks on average.

Age: Minimum 18. Some projects available for 16- and 17-year olds.

Qualif.: No particular skills required.

Work: Building restoration and conservation; 6hrs/day (Monday to Friday).

Lang.: Mostly English; some projects require German.

Accom.: Self-catered basic accommodation. A common room for sleeping and eating. Sleeping may be on the floor or in tents (varies with each project). Bring a sleeping bag and mat.

Cost: Registration fee: GB£150. Room & board included. Travel and personal expenses not included.

Applic.: Application online or by post.

Notes: Projects in Latin America, Asia and Africa require a preparation weekend in Brighton; contact the office for more info. Bring seasonal clothing, working clothes, shoes, gloves, etc. See also: Alliance of European Voluntary Service Organisations; UNESCO.

Copped Hall Trust Archaeological Project

c/o Mrs P M Dalton
Roseleigh, Epping Road, Epping
Essex CM16 5HW UK
Tel: ++44 (1992) 813 725
E-mail: pmd2@ukonline.co.uk
www.weag.org.uk

Desc.:	The project is investigating Old Copped Hall, the site of a courtyard grand house demolished in 1750 that had belonged to Queen Elizabeth's Chancellor Sir Thomas Heneage. The site was not subsequently built upon. Work since 2001 has revealed good survival of remains, extending back to Saxon, Roman and Iron Ages.
Per.:	Possibly mid 13th to late 16th centuries.
Country:	United Kingdom.
Loc.:	Essex, between Epping and Waltham Abbey.
Travel:	Easy access from London or Stansted. Details provided upon application.
Dur.:	2-3 weeks; August.
Age:	Minimum 18.
Qualif.:	Field School: previous experience of digging and recording on an archaeological site is essential. Training Dig: no previous experience is needed. Check website to see which of these 2 programmes is offered in a given year.
Work:	Excavation, keeping field records, processing finds, surveying (magnetometry, resistivity and ground-penetrating radar).
Lang.:	English.
Accom.:	Many hotels and B&Bs available nearby. Lunch and other refreshments during workday provided at no extra cost to all taking part. Good facilities on site include flushing toilets.
Cost:	UK£100 per week. Tools (except trowel) provided.
Applic.:	Online application form or via e-mail or post to Mrs Dalton.

Cornell Halai and East Lokris Project

Department of Classics, Cornell University
120 Goldwin Smith Hall, Ithaca
New York 14853 USA
Tel.: ++1 (607) 255 3354 /255 8328
Fax: ++1 (607) 254 8899
E-mail: jec13@cornell.edu   http://halai.arts.cornell.edu/

Desc.:	The ancient acropolis of Halai, in the present seaside town of Theologos, Greece, was located near major land and sea routes in antiquity, and its well preserved remains are easily accessible today.
Per.:	Neolithic, Archaic, Hellenistic, Bronze Age, Classical, Late Roman or Byzantine.
Country:	Greece.
Loc.:	Theologos, about 75mi (120km) north of Athens, in Lokris (a district in the province of Phthiotis).
Travel:	About 2 hours by bus from Athens (ATH).
Dur.:	4-6 weeks; June to August.
Age:	Minimum 18.
Qualif.:	No previous experience necessary.
Work:	Description and recording of artefacts; study and conservation of the site.
Lang.:	English.
Accom.:	Tents with facilities in Vivos, 2mi (3km) from the site.
Cost:	No cost; room & board provided. Travel expenses not included.
Applic.:	E-mail a brief description of previous experience.

Cotravaux

11 Rue de Clichy
75009 Paris France
Tel.: ++33 (1) 4874 7920
Fax: ++33 (1) 4874 1401
E-mail : informations@cotravaux.org
www.cotravaux.org

Desc.:	Cotravaux coordinates French workcamps. Its role is to promote voluntary work and community projects concerning environmental protection, monument restoration and social projects. Many workcamps operate in different regions of France. Many organisational members of Cotravaux work with foreign partners.
Per.:	Various.
Country:	Projects all over Europe, Asia, America and Africa.
Loc.:	Various.
Travel:	Enquire with the organisation of choice.
Dur.:	2-3 weeks; year round but mainly June to October.
Age:	Minimum 14.
Qualif.:	No experience necessary. Learning and physically disabled volunteers accepted.
Work:	Conservation, archaeology, architecture, heritage, environmental or reconstruction projects. Enquire with organisation of choice.
Lang.:	French, English, Spanish.
Accom.:	Typically tent camps.
Cost:	Volunteers pay for their own transportation to the camps. Room & board included (some camps require a daily contribution).
Applic.:	Contact Cotravaux by fax or mail to obtain the list of partner workcamps in France or other specific countries.
Notes:	A list of Cotravaux member organisations can be obtained through the website: www.cotravaux.org.

Council for British Archaeology

Council for British Archaeology or Young Archaeologists' Club
St Mary's House, 66 Bootham
York YO30 7BZ UK
Tel.: ++44 (1904) 671 417
E-mail: info@britarch.ac.uk
www.britarch.ac.uk/cba/factshts.html

Desc.: The Council for British Archaeology (CBA) publishes British Archaeology 6 times a year, which contains news on topics of archaeological interest. The magazine incorporates "Briefing," which carries advanced information about sites in Britain where volunteers are needed, with brief details of period and nature of the site, location, dates, accommodation, etc., to enable volunteers to plan ahead and book places to work. Most digs occur during the summer months and there is usually (though not always) a minimum age limit of 16 years. Briefing also has information about archaeological courses, conferences, tours and training excavations. The "Briefing" text can also be accessed on the CBA's website and includes links to other web pages, which give details of fieldwork projects. In addition, the CBA publishes a free factsheet series. Especially useful for those starting out is "Everything you always wanted to know about archaeology but were afraid to ask" (Factsheet 8). Factsheets are also available on the CBA website.

Notes: The Young Archaeologists' Club, for the 8-16 age group, is also run under the auspices of the CBA. Over 16s can convert to CBA student membership. Current CBA membership rates are: GB£29 (individual), GB£17 (student) and GB£37 (family, including membership of the Young Archaeologists' Club).

Crow Canyon Archaeological Center

23390 CR K, Cortez
Colorado 81321 USA
Tel.: ++1 (970) 565 8975 /(800) 422 8975 (toll free in North America)
Fax: ++1 (970) 565 4859
E-mail: travel@crowcanyon.org
www.crowcanyon.org

Desc.: This organisation offers adults, youths and schools the opportunity to participate in archaeology through a variety of programmes. The Center involves the public in the study of archaeology and Native American cultures. Volunteers may participate in long-term research on the ancestral Pueblo Indians by working with professional archaeologists in excavation and lab work.

Per.: Basketmaker through Pueblo periods in the South-west.

Country: United States.

Loc.: Cortez, Colorado.

Travel: Details provided upon application.

Dur.: 1 week; June to September.

Age: Minimum 18, except family excavation and week-long programmes for middle school and high school students providing a good introduction to the archaeology of the Southwest. An intensive 3-week summer field school is available for older teens.

Qualif.: No experience necessary.

Work: Excavation, artefact analysis and lab programmes.

Lang.: English.

Accom.: Room & board provided on campus.

Cost: US$1,175-1,400/week including room & board. Travel expenses not included.

Applic.: Online form.

Notes: Academic credit available through the Adams State College (additional tuition fees). International archaeological vacations are also organised.

CVE — Caribbean Volunteer Expeditions

P.O. Box 388, Corning
New York 14830 USA
Tel.: ++1 (607) 962 7846
E-mail: ahershcve@aol.com
www.cvexp.org

Desc.: Caribbean Volunteer Expedition members measure and document historical plantations, windmills and other structures to help local agencies keep a record of their architectural heritage. Projects include historic building surveys, historic cemetery inventories, measurements and photographs of ruins.

Per.: Various.

Country: Throughout the Caribbean, including the Bahamas, Virgin Islands, St. Kitts, Nevis, Antigua, Puerto Rico, Grenada, St. Vincent, Dominica, Trinidad and Tobago, Surinam and Guyana.

Loc.: Various.

Travel: Details provided upon application.

Dur.: Typically 1 week.

Age: Minimum 18.

Qualif.: No experience necessary. Volunteers may perform architectural surveys and drawings, mapping and plan development, stabilize ancient ruins, restore historical buildings, create visitor centres, help to develop and prepare exhibits and interpretive material, work on the conservation and cataloguing of collections and artefacts, prepare exhibit areas and improve public access.

Work: Most work days are half spent in the field.

Lang.: English.

Accom.: Local hotels, houses or campgrounds.

Cost: Varies with each expedition. Volunteers pay for their own travel, room & board, plus an administrative fee to CVE.

Applic.: Call or e-mail the organisation.

Czech American Archaeological Field School in Pohansko

College of DuPage
Well Blvd, Glen Ellyn, Illinois 60187-6599 USA
Tel.: ++1 (630) 942 2022
E-mail: staeck@cod.edu
www.cod.edu/people/faculty/staeck

Desc.: This project studies the origins of the Czech people, culture and state. Students participate in ongoing archaeological excavations exploring the Pohansko enclosure, the structure of the wall and the near "acropolis", as well as plots that may have belonged to the warriors on the site. Also, around 400 burials have been identified within the enclosure.

Per.: Early Medieval, 9th to 10th centuries AD.

Country: Czech Republic.

Loc.: Breclav, south-eastern Czech Republic (Moravia), 3 hours east of Prague (PRG).

Travel: Details provided upon application.

Dur.: 5 weeks; May to June.

Age: Minimum 18.

Qualif.: No experience necessary.

Work: Excavation, mapping, recording of materials.

Lang.: English.

Accom.: On site, in modern and clean trailers.

Cost: To be confirmed, around US$3,233. Room & board (3 meals/day, 5 days/week) included. Airfare and weekend excursions not included.

Applic.: Online form.

Notes: Contact Dr. John P. Staeck, Director, Czech-American Archaeological Field School.

Discovering Italy's Ancient Roman Coast

Earthwatch Institute
Mayfield House,
256 Banbury Road, Oxford OX2 7DE UK
Tel: ++44 (1865) 318 831 - Fax: ++44 (1865) 311 383
E-mail: info@earthwatch.org.uk
www.earthwatch.org/europe

Desc.: This project aims to fill key gaps in our knowledge of the industrial history and coastal economy of Populonia and its region, from the early Roman period to the early Middle Ages. The project results will offer a more profound understanding of the industrial aspects of Roman rule and territorial exploitation, given the site's strategic position near natural resources. Volunteers have a chance to help the research employing skills from all relevant archaeological and historical disciplines to reconstruct the area's complex past as fully as possible.

Per.: Early Roman to early Middle Ages.

Country: Italy.

Loc.: Poggio del Molino, Rimigliano Coastal Park, Tuscany.

Travel: Contact the organisation for details.

Dur.: 13 days; May, June, September and October.

Age: Minimum 18.

Qualif.: No special skills or experience required.

Work: Excavating, documenting all finds, collecting organic samples with a palaeobothanist, surveying the area to collect, clean and document artefacts such as pottery shards, metal and coins.

Lang.: English.

Accom.: Comfortable apartments in the village of Populonia, 5km (3.2mi) away from the site, with all necessary and modern amenities.

Cost: GB£1,395.

Applic.: Online form.

Dispilio Excavations

Aristotle University of Thessaloniki
52057 Dispilio, Kastoria Greece
Tel.: ++30 (24670) 853 32
Fax: ++30 (24670) 859 20
E-mail: dispilioexcavations@hist.auth.gr
http://web.auth.gr/dispilio/

Desc.:	Dispilio is one of the most important Neolithic sites in the Aegean and the first prehistoric lakeside settlement to be excavated in Greece. Research started in 1992 and each year students from the Aristotle University of Thessaloniki, as well as from other Greek Universities, have been trained on excavation and artefact recording techniques by a scientific team consisting of field excavators, palaeobotanists, artefact specialists, conservators, architects, etc.
Per.:	Neolithic.
Country:	Greece.
Loc.:	Dispilio, Lake Orestiada, Kastoria Prefecture, Macedonia, Greece.
Travel:	Details provided upon application.
Dur.:	Minimum 2 weeks; July or September.
Age:	Minimum 18.
Qualif.:	No experience necessary.
Work:	Excavation procedure, artefact recording and conservation, informative lectures, guided tours, pottery lessons and social activities.
Lang.:	English.
Accom.:	Apartment-style residences, 4 people/room, with full kitchen and bath facilities.
Cost:	EUR350/week plus EUR50 for registration and booking; 1 meal/day included (Monday to Saturday).
Applic.:	Online form.

Earthwatch Institute

Mayfield House
256 Banbury Road,
Oxford OX2 7DE UK
Tel.: ++44 (1865) 318 831
E-mail: projects@earthwatch.org.uk
www.earthwatch.org/europe

Desc.:	Earthwatch Institute is an international charity that supports 61 environmental research projects in 31 countries by providing funds and volunteers who contribute financially as well as work alongside leading field scientists and researchers. Volunteers work as part of an international team of people. Earthwatch preferentially funds projects that fit the focus of 1 or more of the following priority research areas: sustainable resource management, climate change, oceans and sustainable cultures.
Per.:	Various.
Country:	Worldwide.
Loc.:	Various.
Travel:	Set meeting points are established for each project. Usually at the nearest international airport.
Dur.:	5-16 days; year round.
Age:	Minimum 18, unless participating on special teen or family team.
Qualif.:	No specific qualifications.
Work:	Various aspects of field and laboratory work.
Lang.:	English.
Accom.:	Anything from tent camping to hotels.
Cost:	Approximately GB£850-1,995, including room & board, training, emergency medical evacuation and the offsetting of greenhouse gas emissions. Grants are available for teachers.
Applic.:	E-mail or telephone for more information. Offices worldwide.

Eco-Archaeological Park Pontecagnano Faiano

Legambiente
Via Salaria 403, 00199 Rome Italy
Tel.: ++39 (06) 8626 8323
Fax: ++39 (06) 2332 5776
E-mail: volontariato@legambiente.eu
www.legambiente.eu/volontariato/campi

Desc.: The camp will take place in the eco-archaeological Pontecagnano Faiano park, which hosts Etruscan ruins and an orchard equipped with picnic tables.

Per.: 6th century BC.

Country: Italy.

Loc.: Pontecagnano, Salerno.

Travel: By train from Naples or Salerno.

Dur.: 10 days; year round.

Age: Minimum 18.

Qualif.: No experience necessary.

Work: Volunteers will maintain the area, from cleaning weeds and painting the Welcome Centre located inside. They will also collaborate in organising the park "Bright Night," which will take place on the 9thAugust, the night of falling stars. The beautiful surroundings, such as Paestum, Pompeii, the Cilento park or the Amalfitana coastline, can also be visited.

Lang.: Italian.

Accom.: School.

Cost: EUR190 plus membership fee.

Applic.: Inquire for instructions. See also: Legambiente.

El Pilar Archaeological Reserve for Maya Flora and Fauna

BRASS El Pilar Program
420 Settlers Valley Drive, Pflugerville, Texas 78660 USA
Fax: ++1 (805) 893 2790 (University of California)
E-mail: ford@marc.ucsb.edu
www.marc.ucsb.edu; www.espmaya.org; www.mayaforestgardeners.org

Desc.:	Advanced projects in a number of areas including archaeology, ecology, plant and wildlife biology, history, agriculture and community development.
Per.:	800 BC to 1000 AD.
Country:	Belize.
Loc.:	Cayo District, north of San Ignacio, on the western border.
Travel:	Details provided upon application.
Dur.:	2 weeks; April to June.
Age:	Minimum 18.
Qualif.:	Volunteers and students in good physical shape may apply. Experience is preferred, but not required.
Work:	Ceramics, drafting, computer work, photography or fieldwork may be involved.
Lang.:	English; Spanish is helpful.
Accom.:	Modern accommodations with bathroom and shower.
Cost:	US$2,500; room & board (Monday to Saturday) and local transport included. Travel expenses and Sunday meals not included.
Applic.:	Online form. Deadline end of February.
Notes:	Coordinated with ISBER/MesoAmerican Research Center at the University of California, Santa Barbara, California 93106 USA. Dr. Anabel Ford, Director.

Elix — Conservation Volunteers Greece

Veranzerou 15, 10677 Athens
Attica Greece
Tel.: ++30 (210) 382 5506
Fax: ++30 (210) 381 4682
E-mail: communication@elix.org.gr
www.elix.org.gr

Desc.:	Summer workcamps in Greece and abroad, with the aim to protect the environment, preserve cultural heritage and promote culture and social services. Intercultural exchanges and conservation work allow young people to contribute to a hosting community.
Per.:	Various.
Country:	Greece.
Loc.:	Varies with project; usually remote areas.
Travel:	Details provided for each project.
Dur.:	2-3 weeks; summer.
Age:	Minimum 18.
Qualif.:	No experience necessary.
Work:	Restoration of traditional buildings, ancient cobbled-stone footpaths and help in archaeological digs; 5-6hrs/day, 6 days/week.
Lang.:	English.
Accom.:	Modest facilities, usually in schools and community or youth centres. Bring a sleeping bag and mat. Household chores involved.
Cost:	Approximately EUR120 (approximately GB£80/US$130).
Applic.:	Online form.

Excavations at Kalavasos-Kokkinoyia

Kalavasos Village
Larnaca District, 7733
Cyprus
E-mail: joanne.clarke@uea.ac.uk
www.uea.ac.uk/art/kalavasos

Desc.:   The site of Kalavasos-Kokkinoyia is situated close to the south coast of Cyprus. Its name arises from its location in fields belonging to the modern village of Kalavasos, the toponym Kokkinoyia referring to the red soil of the locality (Greek *kokkinos*=red). Kokkinoyia is a settlement of the Late Neolithic period (4500-3800 BC), a period otherwise known as the Ceramic or Pottery Neolithic since it follows (with an hiatus) the Aceramic, Pre-pottery or Early Neolithic period (ca. 8000-5500 cal. B.C.) in Cyprus. The Cypriot Late Neolithic is also sometimes referred to as the Sotira culture, named after the first site of this period to be extensively excavated. The period is succeeded by the Early Chalcolithic period (3800-3500 cal. B.C), and ceramics and other aspects of material culture indicate a large measure of continuity between the two periods. Kokkinoyia is characterised by pits and underground chambers and tunnels, which to date do not seem to be associated with a settlement. Work will resume on the chamber and tunnel complex in order to establish what it was used for in Neolithic times.

Per.:   4500-4000 BC.

Country: Cyprus.

Loc.:   2km from Kalavasos village in the south of the island.

Travel: Air to Cyprus then taxi to Kalavasos village.

Dur.:   4 weeks; April.

Age: Minimum 18; maximum 75 or older if fit.

Qualif.:   No previous experience necessary.

Work: On-site training covers the correct use of instruments and tools, identification and retrieval of stratigraphic units (SU), examination and classification of finds (pottery, lithics, floatation), archaeological drawing, survey, and graphical reconstruction.

Lang.: English, Greek.

Accom.: Lodging in tourist style accommodation with hot water showers and cooking facilities. On-site lunches provided.

Cost: GB£700 including on-site lunches and accommodation.

Applic.: Deadline for registration January 31st. See website for details.

Excavations at St Mary Magdalen Leper Hospital, Winchester

Department of Archaeology, The University of Winchester
Sparkford Road, Winchester
Hampshire, SO22 4NR UK
Tel./Fax: ++44 (1962) 827 333
www.provincia.venezia.it/archeove/inglese

Desc.:   A project to examine the remains of the Medieval leper hospital of St Mary Magdalen. Excavation work hopes to reveal more about the history and development of the site and gain an insight into the lives of the people who lived there.

Per.:   11th to 19th centuries AD.

Country: England, UK.

Loc.:   Just outside Winchester, Hampshire.

Travel: Train to Winchester, or flight to Southampton.

Dur.:   Mid August to mid September.

Age: Minimum 18; maximum 75, or older if fit.

Qualif.:   No previous experience necessary.

Work: Onsite training on the use of instruments and tools, recovery and recognition of artefacts and recording of stratigraphic units.

Lang.:   English.

Accom.:   Local campsite, hotel/B&B in Winchester or at the University.

Cost: EUR85 or GB£70/week; accommodation not included.

Applic.:   Limited spaces. Application form on request. Deadline for registration June 30th.

Falerii — Via Amerina

Gruppi Archeologici d'Italia
Via Baldo degli Ubaldi 168, 00167 Rome Italy
Tel./Fax: ++39 (06) 3937 6711
E-mail: segreteria@gruppiarcheologici.org
www.gruppiarcheologici.org;
www.gruppoarcheologico.it

Desc.:	The Roman street Via Amerina and the tombs in the necropolis of the nearby city of Falerii Novi comprise this monumental site, one of the most important giving historical evidence of the Agro Falisco. The site goes nearby the city of Corchiano, the ancient Fescennium, according with some archaeologists.
Per.:	Roman; 3rd century BC to 3rd century AD.
Country:	Italy.
Loc.:	Corchiano (Viterbo), about 40mi (60km) north of Rome.
Travel:	Details provided upon application. Participants must arrive Monday at 18:00 and leave Sunday at 10:00.
Dur.:	1-2 weeks.
Age:	Minimum 18.
Qualif.:	No experience necessary.
Work:	Excavation, survey and documentation for a larger project encompassing the whole layout of Via Amerina, in order to create an environmental-archaeological park in the area.
Lang.:	Italian, English.
Accom.:	Rooms with bunks and bathrooms.
Cost:	EUR260/week; EUR375/2-week session.
Applic.:	Participants must be members of the Gruppi Archeologici d'Italia. Membership fee of EUR35 (including insurance and subscription to the magazine Nuova Archeologia) can be paid at a local office or at the National office at the above address.
Notes:	Bring work boots and gloves, clothes, a water bottle, hat and sleeping bag. See also: Gruppi Archeologici d'Italia.

Farnese — Rofalco

Gruppi Archeologici d'Italia
Via Baldo degli Ubaldi 168, 00167 Rome Italy
Tel./Fax: ++39 (06) 3937 6711
E-mail: segreteria@gruppiarcheologici.org;
etruschi.lamone@gmail.com
www.gruppiarcheologici.org; www.gruppoarcheologico.it

Desc.:	The Etruscan settlement of Rofalco is on a spit of tuff (a mineral deposit) dominating the valley of the Olpeta. It was protected by the rugged nature of the area and by powerful walls with lookout towers. The programme of the Archaeological Campaign of research is part of a project that aims to excavate the rich monumental evidence of that area.
Per.:	Etruscan; 4th to 3rd centuries BC.
Country:	Italy.
Loc.:	Selva del Lamone (forest of Lamone), near Farnese in the Province of Viterbo, about 50mi (80km) north of Rome.
Travel:	Details provided upon application. The sites are easily reachable by bus or train from Rome. Participants must arrive on Sunday at 18:00 and leave on Sunday at 10:00.
Dur.:	1-2 weeks; August.
Age:	Minimum 16.
Qualif.:	No experience necessary.
Work:	Excavation, documentation, survey, restoration lab, etc.
Lang.:	Italian, English, French.
Accom.:	At the Centro GAR of Ischia di Castro (VT), near Farnese. Rooms with bunks and shared bathrooms.
Cost:	EUR240/week; EUR350 for 2 weeks.
Applic.:	Participants must be members of the Gruppi Archeologici d'Italia. Membership fee of EUR35 (see: Falerii project).
Notes:	See: Falerii project and Gruppi Archeologici d'Italia.

Field School in East-Central Europe

Thompson Rivers University
PO Box 3010 Kamloops, BC V2C 5N3 Canada
Tel.: ++1 (250) 828 5182
E-mail: dscheffel@tru.ca
www.tru.ca/europe/field_course.htm

Desc.: This excursion offers the opportunity to make contact with the Roma (Gypsy peoples). Destinations include Presov, a small city with a largely rural society still relatively untouched by Western values. The focus here will be on the sizable population of Roma who live dispersed in dozens of poverty-stricken rural settlements.

Per.: Modern.

Country: Czech Republic, Bosnia-Herzegovina, Montenegro, Slovakia, Ukraine.

Loc.: Prague, Presov, Svinia (an isolated mountain village) and Vilshinki (an ethnic ghetto).

Travel: Contact the organisation for travel details.

Dur.: 4 weeks; May.

Age: Minimum 18.

Qualif.: No experience necessary; non-students accepted space permitting.

Work: Independent field research.

Lang.: English.

Accom.: Various: university residences, simple hotels and local types of housing. Living conditions may vary throughout the trip.

Cost: Inquire for current season. Course-related travel in Europe, shared accommodation and some meals included. Visa fees, airfare, course material, insurance not included.

Applic.: Official course application required. Contact Dr. David Scheffel for information. See also the Svinia Project at www.roma.sk.

Fiji's Ancient Seafarers

Earthwatch Institute
Mayfield House, 256 Banbury Road,
Oxford OX2 7DE UK
Tel: ++44 (1865) 318 831 - Fax: ++44 (1865) 311 383
E-mail: info@earthwatch.org.uk
www.earthwatch.org/europe

Desc:	The first humans to live on these tropical islands more than 3,000 years ago were the Lapita people, the most accomplished seafarers of their time. They routinely crossed more than 900mi (1,500km) of ocean long before people in other parts of the world had sailed that far. Their earliest human settlement in Fiji is on Bourewa Beach. Volunteers help excavate this site and explore others nearby to help understand the cultural history of the region.
Per.:	Lapita era (1200-700 BC).
Country:	Fiji.
Loc.:	Nadi, Viti Levu Island.
Travel:	Contact the organisation for travel details.
Dur.:	15 days; January and February.
Age:	Minimum age 18.
Qualif.:	No special skills or experience required.
Work:	Volunteers and Pacific Islander University students excavate at Bourewa Beach and other nearby sites. They may also search out other sites and use additional archaeological techniques.
Lang.:	English.
Accom.:	Billeting in homes of families within the village of Vusama, with shared bedrooms, or on mattresses in the local community hall.
Cost:	GB£1,395.
Applic.:	Telephone or online form.

FIYE — International Youth Exchange Foundation

Meissnera 1 / 3 lok.319
03-982 Warszawa Poland
Tel.: ++48 (22) 466 5680 - Fax: ++48 (22) 211 2080
E-mail: fiye@fiye.info
www.fiye.pl

Desc.: These camps involve working in areas of archaeological importance to help excavate and preserve sites; intercultural exchanges between participating countries, focusing on similarities and differences in lifestyle, cultural events and icons; or the organisation of and involvement in specific cultural events including historic, religious and artistic festivals.

Per.: Various.

Country: Worldwide.

Loc.: Various.

Travel: Details upon application.

Dur.: Minimum 2 weeks; maximum 12 months.

Age: 18-25.

Qualif.: No experience necessary.

Work: Cultural work, environment preservation, children's activities, construction, renovation, education and intercultural exchanges.

Lang.: English or language of host country.

Accom.: Basic but varies with project.

Cost: Inquire with host organisation.

Applic.: Select a project through the website and contact the host organisation.

Footsteps of Man

Archaeological Cooperative Society "Footsteps of Man"
Piazzale Donatori di Sangue 1
25040 Cerveno BS Italy
Tel.: ++39 (0364) 433 983 - Fax: ++39 (0364) 434 351
E-mail: orme@rupestre.net; fossati@numerica.it
www.rupestre.net/orme/

Desc.:	The project consists of research, drawing and cataloguing the surfaced rocks. There are many stages: research on the site, with excursions to find as yet undiscovered engraved rocks; analysis of damage to the rock surfaces and conservation problems; drawing the engravings onto plastic sheets; paper and digital cataloguing of the engravings.
Per.:	Neolithic.
Country:	Italy.
Loc.:	Paspardo and Valcamonica, province of Brescia, northern Italy. The site is in Paspardo and other areas in Valcamonica.
Travel:	Meeting point at the bus stop of Ceto-Cerveno in Valcamonica, to be confirmed prior to arrival. Bus from the Sesto Marelli station in Milan or train from the National Railway station in Brescia to the station of Ceto-Cerveno.
Dur.:	Minimum 7 days; July to August.
Age:	Minimum 16.
Qualif.:	Archaeologists, scholars, students and enthusiasts welcome.
Work:	Excursion, analysis, drawing and cataloguing.
Lang.:	English and Italian.
Accom.:	House in Paspardo with lab, dormitories, showers and kitchen.
Cost:	EUR400/session (7-days), paid upon arrival. Room & board, working material and transport to the work site included.
Applic.:	Online form. Send deposit of EUR50 (for 1 week) or EUR100 (for 2 weeks) through bank transfer (request bank information).

Fort Garland Field School in Historical Archaeology

Adams State College, Department of HGP
208 Edgemont Blvd.
Alamosa, CO 81102 USA
Email: dick_goddard@adams.edu
www.adams.edu/academics/fieldschool

Desc.: Although Fort Grland was not the site of any major battles, it played major roles in the settlement of the American West. It was constructed to control Indian raids in the area; it was a base of operations for volunteers involved in the two major Civil War battles in the region; it was commanded for a period by Kit Carson and was the duty station of other American military leaders; it was the home of "Buffalo Soldiers" (African American troops); and it was the base of operations for the Ute (Indian) Campaign.

Per.: 1858 – 1883.

Country: United States.

Loc.: Fort Garland, Colorado.

Travel: Fly to Alamosa, Colorado; transportation to the site will be provided. Otherwise fly to Colorado Springs, Colorado or Albuquerque, New Mexico and drive to site.

Dur.: 3, 10-day sessions from June 15th to July 22nd. Volunteers may attend for any portion of the field school.

Age: Minimum 18. 12 if accompanied by a parent or guardian.

Qualif.: No previous experience necessary

Work: Volunteers will receive the same training as students depending on when they arrive. Training includes basic excavation techniques and various technological applications in archaeology such as Global Positioning Systems (GPS), electronic survey recording, Geographic Information Systems (GIS), LIDAR, and various geophysical techniques. Training in basic laboratory procedures and artifact identification is also included. Historical reenactors also provide instruction in historical context.

Lang.:   English.

Accom.:   Participants stay in their own tents. A kitchen, dining room, restrooms, and showers are provided. Participants provide their own food.

Cost: No cost. Participants provide their own camping equipment and food.

Applic.:   A volunteer application will be available on the website after January 1st, or contact via e-mail. No deadline although spaces for volunteers are limited.

"Frescoes Hunting" Photo Expedition to Medieval Churches of Western Bulgaria

Balkan Heritage (BH) Field School
204 Sveta Troica str., BG-6004 Stara Zagora Bulgaria
Tel.: ++359 (42) 235 402 /888 165 402
E-mail: balkanheritage@gmail.com
www.bhfieldschool.org

Desc.: This expedition documents Medieval frescoes preserved in the abandoned churches and chapels of West Bulgaria. Lectures, workshops and training in south-eastern European Medieval history, Orthodox iconography, fresco restoration and guided sightseeing tours to Sofia and Rila monastery are provided.

Per.: Medieval period: Bulgarian, Byzantine and Serbian (10th to 14th centuries). Late Medieval period: Ottoman (15th to 17th centuries).

Country: Bulgaria.

Loc.: Sofia and West Bulgaria.

Travel: Pick-up from and to Sofia airport (SOF).

Dur.: 2 weeks; May or October.

Age: Minimum 18.

Qualif.: Sketching/drawing skills and basic knowledge in documental photography and relevant academic education in Orthodox iconography, fine arts, art history, archaeology, restoration or architecture.

Work: Database recording, sketching, measuring and making a photographic record.

Lang.: English.

Accom.: Flat provided in a Sofia city hotel, with breakfast and lunch at the sites and dinner in the city.

Cost: About EUR899 (-15% for each subsequent BH project), including educational and fieldwork activities, local transfers, room & board, medical insurance, administrative costs and excursion expenses.

Applic.: Online form at http://www.bhfieldschool.org.

The Gabii Project

The University of Michigan, Kelsey Museum of Archaeology
434 South State Street
Ann Arbor MI 48109 USA
E-mail: gabiiproject@umich.edu
http://lw.lsa.umich.edu/kelsey/research/Excavation/Gabii/

Desc.:	This international, multi-institution archaeological initiative is under the direction of Nicola Terrenato of the University of Michigan. Field research commenced in 2007 with a campaign of magnetometric geophysical survey in order to establish the first archaeological plan of the site and to assess the nature of archaeological deposits. Encouraged by results, the project returned in 2008 to complete the magnetometric survey and to carry out various other geophysical prospects to construct stratigraphic site profiles for Gabii. This fairly complete plan for a substantial part of the urban area is a useful guide for excavations which have been undertaken since 2008.
Per.:	Early Iron Age through Late Roman period.
Country:	Italy.
Loc.:	Site of Gabii (Comune di Monte Compatri).
Travel:	Regional train from Rome.
Dur.:	5 weeks; June 21st to July 25th.
Age:	Minimum 18, maximum 75 or older if fit.
Qualif.:	No previous experience necessary.
Work:	On-site training: use of instruments and tools, identification and retrieval of stratigraphic units, examination and classification of finds, study and processing of finds in archaeological lab.
Lang.:	Italian, English.
Accom.:	Lodging at Hotel Villa Mercede in Frascati, Italy.
Cost:	US$3,600/5 weeks, room, board and local transportation included.
Applic.:	Deadline for application February 15th. See website for details.

Giant Prehistoric Dolmen with Petroglyphs in Dzhubga

Department of Central Asia and the Caucasus, Institute for Study of
Material Culture and History, Russian Academy of Sciences
Dvortsovaya nab 18, Saint-Petersburg 191186 Russia
Tel.: ++7 (812) 911 3685
E-mail: viktor_trifonov@mail.ru   www.dolmens.spb.ru

Desc.: The project aims to study, restore, and eventually present a unique prehistoric megalithic tomb to the public. The fieldwork is to excavate and re-assemble the dolmen and, by means of a systematic survey of the Dzhubga valley, to consider the site within the wider valley environment. This is one of the earliest samples of megalithic ashlar masonry in the Black Sea region.

Per.: Bronze Age (2500-2400 BC).

Country: Russia.

Loc.: Black Sea coast, Tuapse region.

Travel: Flight to Krasnodar city, then bus to Dzhubga where volunteers are met by project leaders.

Dur.: 2 to 4 weeks; August to September.

Age: Minimum 18.

Qualif.: No experience necessary.

Work: Excavation, survey, laboratory work.

Lang.: English.

Accom.: Dormitory-style lodging in Dzhubga village (school building) with shared bathroom. Refrigerators unavailable except under special circumstances. Tent camping during survey trips and excavations on remote megalithic sites.

Cost: US$400/2-week session, room & board and project-related costs included. Transportation to and from Dzhubga, registration fee and personal expenses not included.

Applic.: Online form.

Notes: Project site http://dolmens.spb.ru/.

Gordon's Lodge Fieldschool

County Archaeological Services
22 Stronsa Road London W12 9LB UK
Tel: ++44 (020) 8740 8335 /07710 415 948
E-mail: info@glafs.com
www.glafs.com

Desc.:	The Medieval element comprises the remains of substantial limestone buildings. The exact location of any Romano-British features have yet to be confirmed by excavation, but Roman pottery and a number of types of Roman roof tile have been recovered. Aerial photographs suggest the possible presence of house platforms, burials, Bronze Age and Iron Age enclosures.
Per.:	Prehistoric to Late Medieval; 11th to 14th centuries.
Country:	United Kingdom.
Loc.:	Near the historic village of Grafton Regis, between Milton Keynes and Northampton, about 60mi (95km) northwest of London; on farmland at the Buckinghamshire/Northamptonshire border.
Travel:	Easily accessible from junction 15 of the M1 and 7mi (11km) from Milton Keynes railway station, where pick-up may be arranged.
Dur.:	4 days; June to August.
Age:	Minimum 18.
Qualif.:	No experience necessary. Fieldwork experience welcome.
Work:	Excavation, recording, planning, section drawing, surveying and levelling and post-excavation analysis.
Lang.:	English.
Accom.:	Camping with limited facilities available on site; a list of local B&Bs can be provided.
Cost:	GB£30/day; GB£135/session. Tuition included. Room & board not included. A limited number of places at a concessionary rate for archaeology students at degree level are available.
Applic.:	E-mail or call to request application.

Great Arab Revolt Project

University of Bristol
3 Millers Croft, Copmanthorpe, York, YO23 3TW UK
Tel: ++44 (781) 557 0507
E-mail: susan@gwag.org
www.jordan1914-18archaeology.org

Desc.: A project in southern Jordan, to investigate the history and archaeology of the Great Arab Revolt and the origins of the Hashemite Kingdom of Jordan. The archaeology of the First World War is a growing sub-discipline concerned with the investigation, conservation and public presentation of sites and artefact of this period. Whilst much research has been done on the western front, other theatres of WW1, such as Jordan, have been little explored but offer great potential for research and public engagement with heritage.

Per.: First World War: 1914-18.

Country: Jordan.

Loc.: Southern Jordanian desert, along the Hejaz railway route.

Travel: Flight to Amman airport (ADJ) via Heathrow (LHR).

Dur.: 14 days; November.

Age: Minimum 18 - max. 75 or older if fit.

Qualif.: No previous experience necessary.

Work: On-site training covers the correct use of instruments and tools, archaeological drawing and survey.

Lang.: English.

Accom.: Private en-suite room probably in 3-star hotel.

Cost: Approximately GB£2,200. Room & board, flight between LHR and ADJ, insurance, 2 day-excursions and daily bus transport to/from site included.

Applic.: Contact Susan Daniels; deadline July 15th. See website for details. Max. 20 people.

Greek-Canadian Excavations at Argilos

Centre d'études classiques, Université de Montréal
C.P. 6128, succ. Centre-Ville
Montréal, Qc, H3C 3J7 Canada
Tel./Fax: ++1 (514) 343 6111 #38471
E-mail: Jacques.Y.Perreault@umontreal.ca
www.argilos.org

Desc.:	Argilos is situated on the north Aegean coast, 2.5mi (4km) west of the Strymona delta. It is one of the earliest Greek colonies in this area, founded in 655/54 BC. Excavations conducted by the University of Montreal and the Greek Ephoreia of Kavala have uncovered extensive architectural remains, covering all periods of occupation. The city prospered for some 300 years and was destroyed by Philipp II in 357 BC.
Per.:	Archaic/Classical periods; 7th to 3rd centuries BC.
Country:	Greece.
Loc.:	37mi (60km) east of Thessaloniki, northern Greece.
Travel:	Flight to Thessaloniki, bus to Asprovalta.
Dur.:	2-4 weeks; June and July.
Age:	Minimum 18.
Qualif.:	No previous experience necessary.
Work:	Students participate to all aspects of the archaeological process, including museum study, assisted by trained professionals.
Lang.:	English, French, Greek.
Accom.:	Shared rented apartments in the nearby village of Asprovalta.
Cost:	Full 4-week session CAD$3,000, half session CAD$1,650. Room & board included.
Applic.:	Deadline for registration May 15th. See website for details.

Gruppi Archeologici d'Italia

National Office
Via Baldo degli Ubaldi 168
00167 Rome Italy
Tel./Fax: ++39 (06) 3937 6711
E-mail: segreteria@gruppiarcheologici.org
www.gruppiarcheologici.org

Desc: The Association was founded in 1965 with the aim of contributing to the protection and safeguarding of the Italian cultural heritage. With around 100 offices, it is a member of the National Volunteering Centre, promoter and founder of the "European Forum of Associations for Cultural Heritage" and of Koinè "Federation of the archaeological associations in the Mediterranean basin".

Per: Various.

Country: Italy.

Loc.: South-central Italy.

Travel: Details provided upon application.

Dur.: 2 weeks; summer.

Age: Minimum 15 for some camps; minimum 18 for others.

Qualif.: No experience necessary.

Work: Evaluation, cleaning and excavation with land reconnaissance, archaeological documentation and underwater observation. Other activities include training, conferences and meetings.

Lang.: Italian, English.

Accom.: Local lodgings with bunks and shared bathrooms.

Cost: Varies with each camp; generally EUR350-390, plus EUR33 membership fee (including insurance and subscription to the magazine Archeologia).

Applic.: By telephone, fax or e-mail.

Notes: Bring work boots and clothes, gloves, water bottle, hat, sleeping bag, as well as identification documents, membership card, health certificate and anti-tetanus vaccination certificate.

Hebrew University of Jerusalem

Institute of Archaeology
Mount Scopus Jerusalem 91905 Israel
Tel.: ++972 (2) 588 2403/4
Fax: ++972 (2) 582 5548
E-mail: shoulab@savion.huji.ac.il; ornaa@savion.huji.ac.il
http://archaeology.huji.ac.il/

Desc.:	The Institute of Archaeology, established at the Hebrew University in 1926, is the oldest university department of archaeology in Israel. Research activities at the Institute are based on the archaeological excavations carried out at an average of 15 sites each year, many of them in cooperation with the Israel Antiquities Authority or with museums, universities and research institutes in Israel and abroad.
Per.:	Prehistory to Middle Ages.
Country:	Israel.
Loc.:	Various.
Travel:	Details provided for each project.
Dur.:	Varies with project. 1-6 weeks; June to September.
Age:	Minimum 18.
Qualif.:	No experience necessary.
Work:	Survey, excavation, laboratory work, archiving, etc.
Lang.:	English, Hebrew.
Accom.:	Usually in a kibbutz, but may vary.
Cost:	Varies with project.
Applic.:	Each project is linked through the University website. Contact the project directly to apply.

Heidelberg College Experiential Archaeological Program

Center for Historic and Military Archaeology
Heidelberg College, Tiffin, Ohio 44883 USA
Tel.: ++1 (419) 448 2327 - Fax: ++1 (419) 448 2236
E-mail: dbush@heidelberg.edu
www.johnsonsisland.com

Desc.:	This learning programme is available to all Northwest Ohio and Michigan area primary and secondary schools and conducted at the Johnson's Island Civil War Military Prison Site. Students participate in an actual archaeological study and discover materials related to the daily activities of the former prisoners, learning how scientists search for patterns in material culture to help explore human existence.
Per.:	Mid-19th century.
Country:	United States.
Loc.:	Johnson's Island, Lake Erie, 3mi (5km) from Sandusky.
Travel:	Transportation is the responsibility of the sending school.
Dur.:	1 day; March to June.
Age:	Students from the 5th to 12th grades.
Qualif.:	Teachers are given a manuscript that covers what their students should learn prior to the site excavation.
Work:	Explore the plow zone, collect field specimens, scrape and screen the soil, identify and bag all recovered cultural material.
Lang.:	English.
Accom.:	Students are not housed overnight. Portable toilets are on site.
Cost:	US$375/day in the field per group of students (20-24 students).
Applic.:	Limited opportunities available.
Notes:	Interested adults are accepted to volunteer in the spring and fall: 2 Teacher Workshops and Adult Digs (15 days) in July. Contact Dr. David Bush, Site Director. See also: Heidelberg College Summer Undergraduate Field School.

Heidelberg College Summer Undergraduate Field School

Center for Historic and Military Archaeology
Heidelberg College, Tiffin, Ohio 44883 USA
Tel.: ++1 (419) 448 2327 - Fax: ++1 (419) 448 2236
E-mail: dbush@heidelberg.edu
www.johnsonsisland.com

Desc.:	The historic Johnson's Island Civil War Prison site was chosen as the Union depot of captured Confederate officers in late 1861. The Federal Government leased the island and built a prison designed to hold 2,500 prisoners who left behind a vast historical and archaeological record. Journals, letters, autographs, maps and other documents give insight into what prison life was like, as well as the personal conflicts and hardships encountered among families and friends during the Civil War.
Per.:	Mid-19th century.
Country:	United States.
Loc.:	Johnson's Island, Lake Erie, 3mi (5km) from Sandusky.
Travel:	Specific details provided upon application.
Dur.:	5 weeks; early June to July.
Age:	Minimum 18.
Qualif.:	No experience necessary. Ideal for undergraduate college students or adults interested in gaining intensive field experience.
Work:	Excavation, lab work, transcribing copies of historical documents.
Lang.:	English.
Accom.:	Heidelberg College.
Cost:	US$2,220 plus US$85 laboratory fee (subject to change).
Applic.:	Academic credit available with approval from home university.
Notes:	Contact Dr. David Bush. See also: Heidelberg College Experiential Archaeological Program.

The Helike Project-Archaeological Excavations

The Helike Society
58 Solomou Street
Athens 106 82 Greece
Tel.: ++30 (210) 384 5658 /(693) 702 6588
E-mail: eliki@otenet.gr
www.gaiaocean.geology.upatras.gr

Desc.:	Helike was the principal city in the Achaea region. Numerous cores and archaeological excavations have located ruins of classical buildings, a well-preserved Early Helladic settlement, Mycenaean and Geometric occupation layers and remains of the Hellenistic and Roman town of Helike. The Roman road followed by the traveller Pausanias was also discovered and traced.
Per.:	Classical, Mycenaean/Geometric, Early Helladic, Hellenistic, Roman.
Country:	Greece.
Loc.:	Helike; near the villages Rizomylos and Nikolaiika, about 4mi (7km) south-east of Aigion, southwest shore of Gulf of Corinth.
Travel:	Details from Athens to Nikolaiika provided upon application.
Dur.:	6 weeks; July to August.
Age:	Minimum 18.
Qualif.:	No experience necessary. Instruction is provided but participants do prior reading on the region and the history of ancient Greece.
Work:	Excavation, survey, processing, recording, conservation and geoarchaeology; Monday to Friday.
Lang.:	English.
Accom.:	Hotel Poseidon Beach (double occupancy), Nikolaiika.
Cost:	EUR550/week plus EUR55 application fee. Room & board included. Refundable before May 15th; EUR150 cancellation fee.
Applic.:	Print and mail online form by May 15th. Fees due upon acceptance.
Notes:	Physician's note required by May 15th. Insurance required; tetanus shot recommended. Participation certificates available.

Heraclea Lyncestis Excavation Project

Balkan Heritage (BH) Field School
204 Sveta Troica str.
BG-6004 Stara Zagora Bulgaria
Tel.: ++359 (42) 235 402 /888 165 402
E-mail: balkanheritage@gmail.com
www.bhfieldschool.org

Desc.: The project takes place in the excavation site Heraclea Lyncestis: the ancient city was founded by Phillip of Macedon in the 4th century BC and continued its existence as an important economic and administrative centre up to the 6th century AD. Up to 3 field school sessions are available per year, each including 3 modules: fieldwork related to excavations, educational courses, excursions to nearby sites. All participants will receive a BH certificate specifying fieldwork hours, educational modules and sites visited.

Per.: Hellenistic, Roman, Late Antique; 4th century BC to 6th century AD.

Country: Macedonia.

Loc.: Bitola (south-western region).

Travel: Transfer from the nearest airports of Skopje and Thessaloniki is available. Otherwise, participants may travel by train or bus.

Dur.: 2-6 weeks; June to August.

Age: Minimum 16.

Qualif.: No experience necessary.

Work: Excavation, survey, laboratory work, lectures, workshops.

Lang.: English.

Accom.: Hotel rooms with toilets, showers, air-conditioning, TV, etc.

Cost: EUR899/2-week session (-15% for each subsequent session); tuition, fieldwork activities, room & board, excursions/sightseeing tours/entrance fees, medical insurance and administrative costs included.

Applic.: Online form at http://www.bhfieldschool.org.

Notes: 7% of admission fee supports heritage protection fund activities.

Historical and Social Landscapes of the Greater Yellowstone Ecosystem

Northwest College, Anthropology Department
231 West 6th Street, Powell, Wyoming 82435 USA
Tel.: ++1 (307) 754 6131
E-mail: judson.finley@northwestcollege.edu; scheiber@indiana.edu
http://area.northwestcollege.edu/area/anthropology/2310wy.htm

Desc.: Holistic, field-based program in the social history and human ecology of the north-western High Plains and Middle Rocky Mountains with a special emphasis on the Greater Yellowstone Ecosystem. Sessions will be held at Bighorn Canyon National Recreation Area, documenting domestic architecture along the Bad Pass Trail.

Per.: Archaic to Historic (last 2,500 years).

Country: United States.

Loc.: Near Lovell, Wyoming (Bighorn Basin).

Travel: Details provided upon application.

Dur.: 10 days to 20 days; May to June.

Age: Minimum 18.

Qualif.: No experience necessary.

Work: Archaeological survey, surface feature mapping and recording, excavation, cultural resource management.

Lang.: English.

Accom.: Camping in variable conditions. Bring personal camping gear. Volunteers and students are responsible for themselves on the 4-day breaks between sessions.

Cost: US$332 per 10 day session. Food, lodging, and transportation during the session included. Airfare not included.

Applic.: Contact Judson Finley or Laura Scheiber.

Notes: Academic credit available through Northwest College.

Huari-Ancash Archaeological and Bioarchaeological Project

Centre of Archaeological Pre-Columbian Research/ Pantheon Sorbonne
Paris, France or 104 Impasse Cheret, 94000 Creteil France
Tel.: ++33 (17) 255 820
E-mail: bebel_chavin@yahoo.com
http://arqueologiadeancashenglish.blogspot.com

Desc.:	The project is a fieldschool in archaeology aimed at understanding the lifestyle of the prehispanic population in the Puccha valley in Peru. The project is undertaking archaeological excavations to obtain information about the funeral aspects and ancestral cults. The project is supported by the Archaeological Museum of Huaraz, Instituto Nacional de Cultura, The Municipality of Huari and The Instituto Cultural Rvna.
Per.:	Pre-Columbian.
Country:	Peru.
Loc.:	The Huari province is located in Ancash state in Peru, 350mi (560km) north of Lima, about 9 hours by bus. Huari is located about 80mi (130km) west of Huaraz, the capital of Ancash.
Travel:	Details provided upon application.
Dur.:	2-4 weeks; June to August.
Age:	Minimum 18.
Qualif.:	No experience necessary.
Work:	Excavation, training and guided visits.
Lang.:	English and Spanish.
Accom.:	Hotel and camping.
Cost:	Inquire for details.
Applic.:	Via e-mail to Bebel Ibarra, project director.

Humayma Excavation Project

Classics Department, Queen's University
Kingston, Ontario K7L 3N6 Canada
Tel.: ++1 (613) 533 2745
Fax: ++1 (613) 533 6739
E-mail: reevesb@queensu.ca
www.queensu.ca/classics/breeves/index.htm

Desc.:	Excavation at this Nabataean through Early Islamis site in Jordan has been an ongoing project since 1987. The focus of the work is on a Roman-period community adjacent to a fort and the Nabataean town buried beneath it. The fort is well preserved and among the very few known in the Middle East from this period. It has already yielded impressive architectural remains and artefacts.
Per.:	Roman; 2nd to 4th century.
Country:	Jordan.
Loc.:	Jordan's southern desert, 50mi (80km) north of Aqaba.
Travel:	Details provided upon application.
Dur.:	About 6 weeks; May to June.
Age:	Minimum 18.
Qualif.:	Excavation experience preferred but not essential.
Work:	Excavation.
Lang.:	English.
Accom.:	Shared apartments in Aqaba. Food is basic.
Cost:	Approximately CAD$2,500. Room & board included. Travel expenses and tuition not included.
Applic.:	Deadline December 15th.

Huyro Project

Projects Abroad
Aldsworth Parade, Goring
Sussex BN12 4TX UK
Tel.: ++44 (1903) 708 300 - Fax: ++44 (1903) 501 026
E-mail: info@projects-abroad.co.uk
www.projects-abroad.co.uk

Desc.:	Projects Abroad has a number of Inca Projects in and around the Sacred Valley of Peru, in Huyro. Its placements give volunteers the opportunity to do valuable work in picturesque and historic surroundings. They will be involved in a range of different projects from reconstructing Inca irrigation channels to community work and will experience archaeological discoveries firsthand. Volunteers also help with a major reconstruction project of Inca terracing, run by Projects Abroad through a formal agreement with Peru's national heritage body, the Instituto Nacional de Cultura.
Per.:	Various.
Country:	Peru.
Loc.:	Huyro, Sacred Valley.
Travel:	Projects Abroad can arrange travel for volunteers if they wish. Volunteers are met at the airport by a member of staff.
Dur.:	Minimum 1 month; year round.
Age:	Minimum 17.
Qualif.:	No experience necessary.
Work:	Excavation, community development work and expeditions.
Lang.:	English.
Accom.:	Volunteers stay at a community lodge.
Cost:	Project costs range from GB£1,495.
Applic.:	Online or by telephone.

Idalion Expedition

Lycoming College, AC Box 3
Williamsport, Pennsylvania 17701 USA
Tel.: ++1 (570) 321 4283
E-mail: johnson@lycoming.edu;
Idalion1@aol.com

Desc.:	The city of Idalion, Cyprus, was a centre for the copper trade and housed the ancient cult of the Great Mother and her consort, later known as Venus and Adonis. Excavations focus on the Sanctuary of Adonis and on another sanctuary in the Lower City.
Per.:	Late Bronze Age to Roman; 7th to 12th centuries BC.
Country:	Cyprus.
Loc.:	Dhali, 1hr and 20min drive from the beach and 20min from the capital of Nicosia. Taxis and buses available.
Travel:	Details provided upon application.
Dur.:	7 weeks for students; 2 weeks for volunteers; June to August.
Age:	Minimum 18.
Qualif.:	No experience necessary.
Work:	Field work, lectures, on-site excavation, pottery processing, field note taking and illustrating. Artefacts are processed at the dig house. Sunday to Thursday, 6am to 12pm and 4-7pm. Students attend after-dinner lectures 1-2 times a week.
Lang.:	English.
Accom.:	Dhali village dig houses, walking distance from the site, or at an elementary school. Meals on working days provided.
Cost:	US$550/week or US$3,500 for full 7 weeks for volunteers. Field trips, accommodation and weekday meals included. Travel expenses not included. All costs are subject to change.
Applic.:	Deadline for students May 1st; for volunteers May 20th.
Notes:	Academic credit available through Lycoming College. Contact johnson@lycoming.edu.

Iklaina Archaeological Project

University of Missouri-St. Louis
8001 Natural Bridge Road, St. Louis
Missouri 63121-4499 USA
Tel.: ++1 (314) 516 6241- Fax: ++1 (314) 516 7235
E-mail: cosmopoulos@umsl.edu
www.iklaina.org

Desc.: This project studies the emergence of the complex society and statehood in ancient Greece. Its purpose is to investigate the site of Iklaina, among the district capitals of the ancient kingdom of Pylos, in southwest Peloponnesus, Greece.

Per.: Mycenaean era and Greek Bronze Age; 1600-1100 BC.

Country: Greece.

Loc.: Pylos, in southwest Peloponnesus.

Travel: Students must arrive at Pylos, Greece independently. Contact the project for further instruction.

Dur.: 3 weeks; May to July.

Age: Minimum 18.

Qualif.: The course is designed as an introductory course. No background knowledge necessary and no prerequisites.

Work: Excavation and work with finds at the Pylos museum.

Lang.: English.

Accom.: Hotel in Pylos, in double rooms (single room supplement possible). Classes will be held in a classroom at the hotel.

Cost: US$2,790. Accommodation, most meals, site visits, all travel within Greece and archaeological support included. Airfare, insurance, tuition (for credit or auditing) and personal expenses not included.

Applic.: A non-refundable deposit of US$500 is required by March 16th. Applications (including deposits) will be accepted later if space permits. Balance of travel costs due by May 1st.

Indigenous Archaeology in Australia Field School

Dept of Archaeology, Flinders University of South Australia
GPO Box 2100, Adelaide SA 5001 Australia
Tel.: ++61 (8) 8201 3520 - Fax: ++61 (8) 8201 2784
E-mail: lynley.wallis@flinders.edu.au
*http://ehlt.flinders.edu.au/archaeology/fieldwork/field_schools/i
ndigenous/*

Desc.: This field school is being run collaboratively by staff from Flinders University with the cooperation of local Aboriginal organisations and is designed to prepare students to undertake ethical and culturally sensitive research in Indigenous archaeology. The skills taught include research design, field survey, archaeological site recording and excavation, rock art recording, ethical interactions with Indigenous groups and aspects of heritage management.

Per.: The past 40,000 years.

Country: Australia.

Loc.: Various remote pastoral stations, northwest Queensland (approximately 8-12hrs drive from Townsville).

Travel: Flight to Townsville; 4wd and/or bus to field sites arranged.

Dur.: 20 days; June 22nd to July 11th.

Age: Minimum 18; maximum 75, or older if fit.

Qualif.: No previous experience necessary.

Work: Survey and recording of archaeological sites, including rock art; photography; offset and total station surveying; rock-shelter and open-site excavation; stone-artefact recording.

Lang.: English.

Accom.: Limited facilities include camping (either in a tent or swag) or other rugged conditions (limited water and showers). Camping equipment can be provided upon prior arrangement.

Cost: AUD$900 plus tuition of AUD$3000 tuition for international participants or AUD$1750 for Australian participants. Project costs once in Townsville included. Flights not included.

INEX Slovakia — Association for International Volunteer Exchange

Kosicka 37, 821 09 Bratislava Slovakia
Tel.: ++421 (2) 5564 3030
Fax: ++421 (2) 5564 3031
E-mail: inex@inex.sk
www.inex.sk

Desc.: INEX Slovakia offers several workcamps in various sectors. Amoung their various archaeological workcamps is Black Castle, where the volunteers work on discovering forgotten pages of history within these Medieval ruins. This project is being undertaken by non-profit organisation Cierny Hrad. The main goal is to clean the area of castle ruins and recover sleeping pieces of history.

Per.: Medieval; 8th to 15th centuries.

Country: Slovakia.

Loc.: The Black Castle, near to Zlatno village.

Travel: Flight to Bratislava (BTS), or Vienna (VIE). Bus to Zlatno from the Central Bus Station in Bratislava (Autobusova Stanica Mlynske Nivy).

Dur.: 2 weeks; summer.

Age: Minimum 18.

Qualif.: No experience necessary.

Work: Archaeological work varies year to year but may include survey, excavation and archiving the ruins.

Lang.: English.

Accom.: In tents; volunteers have to bring mat and sleeping bag. Showers are available in village (2km away).

Cost: The partner organisation (see application below) determines costs. INEX will not charge any additional fees.

Applic.: Interested volunteers must apply through a partner organisations within the Alliance of Voluntary Organisations or SCI.

Notes: Volunteers must provide their own insurance. Bring a sleeping bag, mat, flash lamp, raincoat, cutlery, working clothes and working shoes. Besides international workcamps taking place mainly in summer months, INEX also organises trainings for present and future camp leaders, summer camps for children and for students, study visits and other youth activities. INEX Slovakia is a member of the Alliance of European Voluntary Service Organizations (see listing), an official partner of Service Civil International (see listing) and successfully co-operates with organisations associated in Youth Action for Peace (see listing). All activities of INEX Slovakia are supported by the Ministry of Education of the Slovak Republic.

Ingleston Motte Research Project

Stewartry Archaeological Trust
Kingston, Rhonehouse, Castle Douglas, Dumfries and Galloway
Scotland DG7 1SA UK
Tel.: ++44 (1556) 680 478
E-mail: lizzie@sjcresearch.co.uk
www.sat.org.uk

Desc.:	Ingleston Motte is a 12th- to 13th-century Medieval motte hill. Excavation regards a twice-destroyed timber tower and defences and related industrial features.
Per.:	1100-1200 AD.
Country:	Scotland.
Loc.:	Parish of Kelton.
Travel:	By train, coach, car, etc. Travel is the volunteer's responsibility.
Dur.:	July to September.
Age:	No minimum age.
Qualif.:	Previous experience necessary; volunteers must be experienced diggers.
Work:	On-site training covers the correct use of instruments and tools, identification (pottery, numismatics, glass fragments), archaeological drawing, survey, dumpy levelling.
Lang.:	English.
Accom.:	Diggers provide their own accommodation; caravan, camping and B&Bs are available locally.
Cost:	GB£35/week towards dig funds.
Applic.:	Deadline for registration May 31st. See website for details.

International Archaeological Student Camp — Amphaxitis

Institute for Art History and Archaeology, Faculty of Philosophy,
Sts. Cyril and Methodius University
Bul. Krste Misirkov b.b. 1000 Skopje Republic of Macedonia
Tel.: ++389 (2) 311 6520
E-mail: silvana.blazevska@gmail.com   www.vardarskirid.org.mk

Desc.:	The main goal of the Program is better understanding the ancient civilisations in lower Vardar Valley - ancient Amphaxitis, their preservation and presentation to the public. Daily activities offer students the opportunity to learn the methods of archaeological research through active fieldwork. The major current project is the Vardarski Rid Archaeological Project studying all the aspects of everyday life at the ancient town at Vardarski Rid.
Per.:	Late Bronze Age to Early Roman Period; 12th century BC to 1st century AD.
Country:	Macedonia.
Loc.:	Vardarski Rid near town of Gevgelia, southern Macedonia.
Travel:	From Skopje or Thessaloniki airport, bus or train to Gevgelia.
Dur.:	4-5 weeks; June to July.
Age:	Minimum 18.
Qualif.:	No experience necessary.
Work:	Excavation, field documentation, work on the finds.
Lang.:	English.
Accom.:	Motel, about 200m from the site.
Cost:	EUR950 per 4-week session; EUR170 for each subsequent session. Room/board and project-related costs are included. Transportation to and from Gevgelia, airport departure tax and personal expenses not included.
Applic.:	Online form.
Notes:	Academic credits, evening lectures and organised tours to the nearby archaeological sites are available.

Introductory Archaeological Geophysics Field School

Dept. of Archaeology, Flinders University of South Australia
GPO Box 2100, Adelaide SA 5001 Australia
Tel.: ++61 (8) 8201 3520 - Fax: ++61 (8) 8201 2784
E-mail: lynley.wallis@flinders.edu.au
http://ehlt.flinders.edu.au/archaeology/fieldwork/field_schools/g eophysics/index.php

Desc.:	This field school is aimed at graduates in archaeology or with a related background who wish to gain experience in archaeological geophysics. The topic provides students with an understanding of the scientific principles behind a range of techniques used in archaeological prospecting and the basic field operation of such techniques, as well as data processing, data interpretation and geophysical reporting. A series of lectures, demonstrations, practical hands-on sessions and computer-based labs, as well as field sessions at an historic cemetery site in the Adelaide metropolitan area are provided.
Per.:	19th century.
Country:	Australia.
Loc.:	Flinders University campus; various historical cemetery sites in or near the Adelaide metropolitan area.
Travel:	Request direction from Adelaide (ADL) to the university campus.
Dur.:	8 days; September 21st-28th.
Age:	Minimum 18; maximum 75, or older if fit.
Qualif.:	No previous geophysical experience necessary.
Work:	Techniques covered include ground penetrating radar (GPR), electromagnetic induction (EMI), direct current resistance, magnetometer, gradiometer, magnetic susceptibility and a range of marine geophysics (side scan sonar, sub-bottom profiling and swath bathymetry). Hands-on experience for students includes GPR, magnetometer and EMI. Under supervision, participants will be required to carry out a multi-technique geophysical survey of an historical cemetery site in order to locate unmarked graves.
Lang.:	English.

Accom.: Information about nearby accommodation options to suit a range of budgets can be provided upon request.

Cost: AUD$3000 (international participants); AUD $1750 (Australian participants). Transport to cemetery sites included.

Applic.: Deadline September 1st; see website or contact Lynley Wallis for details.

Iron-Age/Celtic Necropolis of Pintia

ArchaeoSpain
PO Box 1331
Farmington, Connecticut 06034 USA
Tel./Fax: ++1 (866) 932 0003
E-mail: programs@archaeospain.com
www.archaeospain.com/pintia

Desc.:	Participants will join the excavation of an Iron Age necropolis that was used by a pre-Roman culture with Celtic roots. Over the past decade, around 150 cremation burials (warriors, women and children) with abundant grave goods have been uncovered, helping to better understand the Vaccean culture.
Per.:	Iron Age, Roman.
Country:	Spain.
Loc.:	Padilla de Duero, Valladolid province.
Travel:	Meet at Madrid airport (MAD) on the first day and drive to the site.
Dur.:	4 weeks; June to September.
Age:	Minimum 18.
Qualif.:	No previous experience necessary.
Work:	Training on use of excavation tools and mapping instruments, identification and retrieval of stratigraphic units (SU), examination and classification of artefacts and archaeological drawing.
Lang.:	English; Spanish helpful. Participants will be immersed in the language daily, therefore it is hoped that they will take advantage and improve their spoken Spanish.
Accom.:	Dorm-style room at research facility.
Cost:	US/Canada: US$2,250/session. Other countries: EUR1,590/session. Meals prepared by local cook, lodging, transfers to/from airport, excursions, medical insurance, application fee, administrative costs included.
Applic.:	Rolling.
Notes:	Academic credit available with approval from home institution.

Ironbridge Gorge Museum Trust
Coalbrookdale
Telford, Shropshire TF8 7DX UK
Tel.: ++44 (1952) 583 003
Fax: ++44 (1952) 588 016
E-mail: online form
www.ironbridge.org.uk

Desc.:   Volunteers are required at this World Heritage site as demonstrators in exhibits, site maintenance and street festivities. Other volunteer opportunities are available at the Museum's many other sites in the valley. The Iron Bridge, built in 1779, is universally recognised as a potent symbol of the Industrial Revolution.

Per.:   18th century.

Country: United Kingdom.

Loc.:   Spanning the River Severn at Ironbridge in Shropshire.

Travel: Details provided upon application.

Dur.:   2 weeks; April to October.

Age: Minimum 18.

Qualif.:   Some historical background is a plus, although training, equipment and supervision are provided.

Work: Museum curation and public education.

Lang.:   English.

Accom.:   No accommodations available. Volunteers are given a luncheon voucher for a full day's work, plus free entry to other Trust sites.

Cost: Museum insurance covers all volunteers.

Applic.:   Applications accepted year round by the Volunteer Co-ordinator, Blists Hill Victorian Town, at the above address.

Notes: Alternative contact is David de Haan, at The Ironbridge Institute, Ironbridge Gorge Museum, Coalbrookdale, Telford, Shropshire TF8 7DX. Tel: ++44 (1952) 432 751, fax: ++44 (1952) 435 937, or e-mail: ironbridge@bham.ac.uk.

Isca Project

Archaeological Group "Paolo Orsi" - Gruppi Archeologici d'Italia
Via Trento e Trieste 118
88068 Soverato CZ Italy
Tel./Fax: ++39 (0967) 220 24
E-mail: studiomaida@virgilio.it
www.gruppiarcheologici.org/ga.soverato

Desc.:	Previous excavations have uncovered several areas with different purposes. The collected artefacts and the geographic location of the study areas may be lead to the supposed presence of a statio (outpost), later turned to dwelling use.
Per.:	1st century BC to 4th century AD.
Country:	Italy.
Loc.:	Isca sullo Ionio, Cosenza, Calabria.
Travel:	Train to Soverato, 30mi (50km) from Lamezia airport.
Dur.:	10 days; June to September.
Age:	Minimum 18.
Qualif.:	No previous experience necessary. Subscription to Gruppi Archeologici d'Italia (which provides insurance) is compulsory.
Work:	Field and laboratory activities, lectures, guided tours and leisure time (the site is adjacent to the seaside) .
Lang.:	English and Italian.
Accom.:	In a primary school, with large rooms, showers and facilities. Traditional food cooked on site.
Cost:	EUR285.
Applic.:	Email the online form along with CV (preferably in Italian); deadline for application: June 30th.

Israel Ministry of Foreign Affairs

www.mfa.gov.il (search for "Archaeological Excavations in Israel ")
See also:
Israel Antiquities Authority (IAA)
Rockefeller Museum Building PO Box 586
Jerusalem, 91004 Israel
www.antiquities.org.il

Desc.:	There are many Universities and organisations throughout Israel listed through the Ministry. Many archaeologists enlist volunteers to help on their digs, as volunteers are highly motivated and wish to learn and gain experience. The Israel MFA features an excellent and updated list in its website possibly listing all excavations in Israel. The government body for archaeology in Israel is the Israel Antiquity Institute, which also manages directly excavations accepting volunteers. See website for details.
Per.:	Various.
Country:	Israel.
Loc.:	Various.
Travel:	Contact project of interest for details. Volunteers are responsible for their own travel arrangements to and from Israel.
Dur.:	Various.
Age:	Minimum 18.
Qualif.:	Usually, no previous experience is necessary. Some expeditions offer credit courses from sponsoring institutions. Informal lectures covering the history and archaeology of the site are often supplemental.
Work:	Often difficult and tedious including digging, shovelling, hauling baskets of earth and sherds, cleaning pottery sherds, etc. Typically the dig begins before dawn and ends after noon with a rest period after lunch. The afternoons and early evenings may be free or devoted to lectures, cleaning and sorting of pottery and other finds. Schedule varies according to the conditions at the site.
Lang.:	English, Hebrew.

Accom.: Varies from sleeping bags in the field, to rooms in hostels or kibbutzim, to 3-star hotels near a site. Excavations conducted in or near a city often require volunteers to find their own accommodations. Volunteers who require kosher food should inquire in advance.

Cost: There is usually a registration fee and a charge for room & board, although on some excavations these are free. All charges listed are in US dollars.

Applic.: Any questions, comments, registration, or requests for additional information must be directed to the contact person indicated for each project and not to the Israel Foreign Ministry. When applying to the director of an excavation, indicate any previous studies in archaeology or related fields, such as anthropology, architecture, geography, surveying, graphic arts; or experience in excavation work, pottery restoration or photography.

Notes: Volunteers should have comfortable, sturdy, weather appropriate clothing for heavy work. Work-gloves, sleeping bag, canteen and towels are often required. Volunteers must arrange for medical and accident insurance in advance. Even in instances when accident insurance is provided, it is strongly advised that volunteers come fully insured, as the insurance offered is minimal. The Israel Ministry of Interior regulations require that passports of all volunteers (other than Israeli) be stamped with a volunteer visa (B4). This request should be made by the volunteer at the point of entry into Israel.

Judith River Dinosaur Institute

PO Box 51177
Billings, MT 59105 USA
Tel./Fax: ++1 (406) 656 5842
E-mail: jrdi@bresnan.net
www.montanadinosaurdigs.com

Desc.:	This project is an opportunity for volunteers to work on the first Jurassic dinosaur graveyard found in Montana.
Per.:	Jurassic and Late Cretaceous.
Country:	United States.
Loc.:	Judith River Formation near Roundup, Montana.
Travel:	From Billings (BIL) drive or bus to motel.
Age:	Minimum 14.
Qualif.:	Experienced amateurs are preferred. This project is for those seriously interested in working on scientific specimens of museum and research quality. Not for the casual vacationer.
Work:	Field excavation, recording and mapping finds, taphonomic interpretation, jacketing and removal of specimens.
Lang.:	English.
Accom.:	Boothill Inn (++1 (406) 245 2000, www.boothillinn.com) on Saturday and Friday evenings; camping for 5 days in the field.
Cost:	US$1,695. Transportation to the field, meals, tools and instruction included. Accommodation and camping equipment not included.
Applic.:	Online form sent via e-mail along with half of the required tuition cost. The deposit is refundable only if cancellations are received no less than 90 days before the departure dates.
Notes:	In rugged terrain and hot climates, participants must be in good physical condition. Pre-existing medical conditions are approved on a case by case basis.

Kabyle Archaeological Survey

Yambol Regional Archaeological Survey
V. Petleshko 75 Sofia 1000 Bulgaria
Tel.: ++359 (889) 482 34
E-mail: adelas@umich.edu

Desc.:	A surface survey project studying the hinterland of the ancient city of Kabyle, Bulgaria. It is a genuinely interdisciplinary project involving specialists in palynology, environmental studies, remote sensing, GIS and database design.
Per.:	Roman.
Country:	Bulgaria.
Loc.:	Kabyle, 56mi (80km) west of the Black Sea, on the Thracian plain, southeast Bulgaria.
Travel:	Flight to Sofia (SOF), then by bus to city of Yambol.
Dur.:	Approximately 6-8 weeks, weather permitting; end February to mid-April. Long term: 2 months in spring and fall.
Age:	Minimum 18. Physical fitness and healthy attitude required.
Qualif.:	No skills or previous experience necessary but welcome with GIS, database operation and survey methodology. Training provided.
Work:	Fieldwalking, intensive systematic surface survey, documentation and processing of finds. Free time and entertainment arranged.
Lang.:	English, German, Buglarian, Italian, Czech, Russian.
Accom.:	Shared rooms at the base, or at the nearby village of Kabyle.
Cost:	No fees. Transport and living costs (range between US$250-400 depending on the arrangement) not included.
Applic.:	Send a CV, outlining education, skills, experiences and dates of availability. Project coordinator: Adela Sobotkova, Research Fellow at American Research Center at Sofia.

Kalat Project

Chapter of Campobello di Licata, Archeoclub d'Italia
c/o Centro Polivalente, Via Trieste 1
92023 Campobello di Licata Italy
Tel./Fax: ++39 (0922) 883 508
E-mail: campi@kalat.org
www.kalat.org

Desc.:	Archaeological, cultural and natural heritage project in southern Sicily, at one of the most interesting archaeological areas in Italy. Over the centuries, the area was occupied by Greeks, Romans, Normans, Swabians, Angevins and Aragonese and is rich in monuments and archaeological sites. Historical pathways for the creation of tourist itineraries are proposed.
Per.:	Neolithic to Byzantine, Islamic and late Middle Ages.
Country:	Italy.
Loc.:	Campobello di Licata, province of Agrigento, Sicily.
Travel:	Various train and bus connections from Catania and Palermo to Campobello di Licata, where the organisation can be called for pick-up. Request directions to arrive by car.
Dur.:	1-2 weeks; July 28th to August 9th and August 18th to August 30th.
Age:	Minimum 18; maximum 30.
Qualif.:	No experience necessary.
Work:	Survey, archaeological research, mapping, public education, environmental recovery, tourist promotion, cultural exchange.
Lang.:	Italian, English.
Accom.:	Hostel in the primary school (Via Carnevale); rooms sleep 8.
Cost:	Request information from the project directly.
Applic.:	Online form. Confirmation of booking will be made upon the receipt of the curriculum and pre-payment of half of the participation fee. The remainder of fees is paid upon arrival.
Notes:	Bring long trousers, boots, hat, flask, torch, sheets, toiletries.

Kansas Archeology Training Program

Kansas Historical Society
6425 SW 6th Ave, Topeka, KS 66615-1099 USA
Tel.: ++1 (785) 272 8681
Fax: ++1 (785) 272 8682
E-mail: vwulfkuhle@kshs.org
www.kshs.org/resource/katphome.htm

Desc.: The KATP offers a unique opportunity to work alongside professional and vocational archaeologists and participate in original research to improve their knowledge of archaeological methods and theory.

Per.: Range of prehistoric and historic period sites.

Country: United States.

Loc.: Kansas.

Travel: Transportation to the site is not provided.

Dur.: 16 days in early June. Any number of days can be attended.

Age: Minimum 10.

Qualif.: No experience necessary.

Work: Participants assist archaeologists in excavating sites, surveying and cleaning/cataloguing artefacts in the lab. They learn related techniques in various courses, useful for college credit.

Lang.: English.

Accom.: Camping and motel facilities are suggested; participants are responsible for making their own arrangements.

Cost: US$20/person for members of the Kansas Anthropological Association or Kansas Historical Society, US$80 for non-members, if registration is submitted by early May deadline. After May deadline, US$30 for members and US$90 for non-members. Transportation, room & board not included.

Applic.: Announcement for June project is made in January, and the registration packet is posted on the web site around March 1st.

Kfar HaHoresh Archaeology & Anthropology Field School

Institute of Archaeology, The Hebrew University of Jerusalem
Mount Scopus Jerusalem 91905 Israel
Tel.: ++972 (2) 588 2403 /4 - Fax: ++972 (2) 582 5548
E-mail: goring@h2.hum.huji.ac.il
www.hum.huji.ac.il/archaeology

Desc.:	The Early Neolithic cultures of this region are the earliest agricultural societies in the world. The Kfar HaHoresh excavations reveal the site to be a unique mortuary and cult centre serving neighbouring lowland village communities. Finds include many human skeletons and secondary burials sealed under lime-plastered surfaces. There is evidence for extensive lime-plaster manufacture at the site; an experimental programme of this early pyrotechnology is being conducted on site.
Per.:	Early Neolithic; 7000 BC.
Country:	Israel.
Loc.:.	In the Nazareth Hills of Lower Galilee, northern Israel.
Travel:	Details provided upon application.
Dur.:	6 weeks; June to August.
Age:	Minimum 18.
Qualif.:	No experience necessary.
Work:	Excavation, recovery, recording and artefact analysis.
Lang.:	English.
Accom.:	Kibbutz Kfar HaHoresh in 2-3 person shared rooms. Meals are in the kibbutz dining room.
Cost:	US$350/2-week session plus US$150 non-refundable registration fee.
Applic.:	Deadline mid-April. Request an application form via e-mail.
Notes:	Academic credit available through the Rothberg International School, Hebrew University with additional fees.

Kinneret Regional Project

University of Bern, Switzerland
University of Helsinki, Finland
University of Leiden, The Netherlands
University of Mainz, Germany
E-mail: stefan.muenger@theol.unibe.ch
www.kinneret-excavations.org

Desc.:	The Kinneret Regional Project is a European expedition to the north-western shore of the Sea of Galilee under the auspices of the Universities of Bern, Helsinki, Leiden and Mainz. The focus of the research is to explore the site of Tel Kinrot (ancient Kinneret) and its environs.
Per.:	Chalcolithic to Byzantine; 4500 BC to 620 AD.
Country:	Israel.
Loc.:	Tel Kinrot and Horvat Kur, about 12km north of Tiberius on the north-western shore of the Sea of Galilee.
Travel:	Details provided upon application.
Dur.:	4 weeks; July to August.
Age:	Minimum 20.
Qualif.:	Qualified students and non-academic volunteers interested in the archaeology and culture of the Southern Levant.
Work:	Survey, excavation, mapping, processing excavated materials, documentation and registration; fieldschool (4 ECTS).
Lang.:	English.
Accom.:	Karei Deshe youth hostel, less than a mile from the site: 4-6 persons per room, provided with showers, A/C, fridge and TV. Private beach at the Lake of Galilee.
Cost:	EUR1,200-1,500 (students get a 50% reduction). Room & board, fieldschool and excursions included (course registration is free of charge). Travel expenses, optional fieldtrips and personal expenses not included. Costs are subject to change.
Applic.:	Via e-mail or online application form by April 1st.

Koobi Fora Field School

Rutgers University
131 George Street, New Brunswick, NJ USA
Tel.: ++1 (732) 932 8083
E-mail: jwharris@ric.rutgers.edu
www.kffs.rci.rutgers.edu

Desc.: Undergraduate and graduate students learn the basic principles of palaeoanthropology "hands on" at one of the most productive and spectacular early hominid regions in the world. The curriculum is driven by an international multi-disciplinary team of researchers. Experts from the National Museums of Kenya, Rutgers University and other universities, provide instruction in lectures, labs and within the context of on-going field projects.

Per.: 2.2 million years ago (Plio-Pleistocene) and Holocene interval of the last 12,000 years.

Country: Kenya.

Loc.: Lake Turkana, northern Kenya.

Travel: Train to Nairobi, then journey to central and northern Kenya.

Dur.: 6 weeks; June and July.

Age: Minimum 18.

Qualif.: No previous experience necessary.

Work: Field-based lecture, laboratory and practical instruction; 7 days/week, 8hrs/day for 3 weeks (approximately 140 hours).

Lang.: English.

Accom.: Camping (tents not supplied) and at base camp on Lake Turkana. The field site is remote and there is little outside communication.

Cost: US$6,000-6,500, depending on residency. In-field costs included.

Applic.: Rolling deadline, see website for details.

Notes: 8 upper division university credits through Rutgers University.

Krastevich — A Greek Emporion in Ancient Thrace

Provias Ltd
Zona B18, bl 3, A6, Sofia Bulgaria
Tel.: ++359 (888) 780088
E-mail: contact@archeobg.org
http://hisar.archeobg.org/

Desc.:	This is an excavation of a settlement from the Classical period. The site represents a Greek commercial outpost in the interior of Ancient Thrace, existed during the 5th century BC. The first 4 years of excavation revealed stone architecture and mixed Graeco-Thracian material culture. Currently 3 buildings and the adjoining street layout are under investigation. A sanctuary with a temple building from the same period is being excavated in the nearby vicinities.
Per.:	Classical period; 5th century BC.
Country:	Bulgaria.
Loc.:	At the footsteps of Sredna Gora Mountains.
Travel:	Airplane or train to Sofia, then bus to Krastevich.
Dur.:	Minimum 2 weeks.
Age:	Minimum 18; maximum 75, or older if fit.
Qualif.:	Basic archaeological skills and knowledge on the period are desirable, though not essential.
Work:	Full engagement in the excavation process. Assisting in the archaeological documentation and the processing of the finds. Lectures and visits to other sites in the region. Several ancient sites in the region, including an amphitheatre in Plovdiv, Starosel Thracian tomb, Roman thermae complex in Hisar, are visited.
Lang.:	English, French.
Accom.:	Lodging in local house, all utilities available.
Cost:	EUR950/2 weeks. Room & board included.
Applic.:	Rolling.

Lahav Research Project, Phase IV: Tell Halif Excavations

Emory University, Dept. of Middle Eastern & South Asian Studies
S-312 Callaway Center, Atlanta GA 30322 USA
Tel./Fax: ++1 (404) 727 7951 /(404) 727 2133
E-mail: oborows@emory.edu

Desc.: This project aims to recover remains from the fortified town destroyed at the end of the 8th century BC, probably by Sennacherib in 701 BC. Main discoveries are domestic structures with household objects and installations strung along the city wall. One major occupation of the inhabitants was textile production, and the question is whether this was developed because of Assyrian economic pressure.

Per.: 8th century BC and later (Persian, Hellenistic) periods.

Country: Israel.

Loc.: Tell Halif, north-east of Beersheba, Southern Israel.

Travel: Pre-arranged pick-up at the Ben Gurion Airport.

Dur.: 5 weeks; June to July.

Age: Minimum 18; no maximum.

Qualif.: 1 year of college; no previous field experience necessary.

Work: 5/6-day weeks. On-site training covers the correct use of instruments and tools, identification and retrieval of stratigraphic units, examination and classification of finds, archaeological drawing. Lectures and workshops. Weekend trips.

Lang.: English.

Accom.: Lodging in kibbutz accommodations with 3 meals/day.

Cost: US$2,235 for room & board; US$8,795 for room & board, trips, insurance and 8 academic credits through Emory University.

Applic.: Deadline for registration February 28th.

Lajuma Archaeological Research Project

P.O. Box 522
Makhado, Limpopo 0920 South Africa
Tel./Fax : ++27 (15) 593 0352
E-mail: stephan@lajuma.com
www.lajuma.com

Desc.: The Lajuma Research Centre provides research and opportunities to students and volunteers from foreign countries and from local disadvantaged communities. Its mission is to build a database of the environment, biodiversity, ecology and archaeology of the area with the assistance of local and international universities. The area is a South African Natural Heritage Site and has an interesting archaeological history and a high cultural diversity.

Per.: Early Stone Age to Late Iron Age.

Country: South Africa.

Loc.: Limpopo, northern South Africa; in a private nature reserve.

Travel: Flight to Pretoria or Johannesburg (JNB), then bus to Louise Trichardt. Further information upon application.

Dur.: Minimum 1 month.

Age: Minimum 18.

Qualif.: No experience.

Work: Mapping and documentation of sites, recording of significant features, analysing artefacts, compiling a photo database of finds.

Lang.: English.

Accom.: Housing equipped with hot showers, flush toilets, a gas stove, fridge, tapped water, washing machine, gas, firewood and electricity (220v, generated at a waterfall and is not suitable for high wattage equipment such as kettles and hair driers).

Cost: R100(about US$15)/day, including lodging and transport from/to the bus terminus in Makhado. Board and airfare not included.

Applic.: Contact Stephan Gaigher at stephan@lajuma.com.

Lamanai Archaeological Project

University of North Carolina Wilmington
Department of Anthropology 601 South College Road
Wilmington, North Carolina 28403-5907 USA
Tel.: ++1 (910) 962 3543
E-mail: simmonss@uncw.edu
http://people.uncw.edu/simmonss/

Desc.: Participants are introduced to ancient Maya material culture, the management of these resources and community involvement with archaeological database and cultural resource management strategies as they pertain to Maya archaeology.

Per.: Pre-Classic to Historic Maya; 1500 BC to 1875 AD.

Country: Belize.

Loc.: Belize, near the town of Orange Walk.

Travel: Details provided upon application.

Dur.: 2 weeks; May to June.

Age: Minimum 18.

Qualif.: No experience necessary.

Work: Process, sort and analyse artefacts including ceramics, lithics and small finds; mapping, laboratory work, community development, lectures and tours. Excavations not involved.

Lang.: English and Spanish.

Accom.: Students will live as resident guests in the Indian Church town.

Cost: Inquire for full costs.

Applic.: Online form.

Notes: Academic credit available with approval from home University.

Legambiente

Via Salaria 403
00199 Rome Italy
Tel.: ++39 (06) 8626 8323
Fax: ++39 (06) 2332 5776
E-mail: volontariato@legambiente.eu
www.legambiente.eu/volontariato/campi

Desc.: This organisation combines the protection of the environment with the restoration and enhancement of cultural heritage. Current projects include restoration and protection camps in small islands near Sicily, underwater archaeology and ecology camps in Sicily, ecological research in the Italian Alps, archaeological study in southern Italy and many others.

Per.: Various.

Country: Italy.

Loc.: Various.

Travel: Details provided with each project.

Dur.: 10-20 days; year round.

Age: Special programmes available for those under 18.

Qualif.: No experience necessary.

Work: Manual labour; restoration, renovation, cleaning, etc.

Lang.: Italian, English.

Accom.: Various accommodations in schools, houses, convents, etc.

Cost: EUR120-240 plus membership fee.

Applic.: Contact the Volunteer office of Legambiente for further information and application forms. See also: Eco-Archaeological Park Pontacagnano Faiano, Necropoli of Pantalica Sortino (Sicily), Villasmundo-Melilli (Sicily).

The Leon Levy Expedition to Ashkelon

Harvard University Semitic Museum
6 Divinity Ave, Cambridge
MA 02138 USA
Tel.:++1 (617) 495 9385
E-mail: leonlevyexpeditiontoashkelon@gmail.com
www.fas.harvard.edu/~semitic/ashkelon

Desc.:	This expedition consists in a dig at the ancient seaport city of Ashkelon, capital of Canaanite kings, harbor of the Philistines, and stomping ground of the biblical hero, Samson. An opportunity to earn college credit while digging in a beautiful national park and favorite Israeli resort area overlooking the Mediterranean Sea.
Per.:	Middle Bronze Age (16th century BC) through Roman Period.
Country:	Israel.
Loc.:	Ashkelon.
Travel:	Fly to Ben-Gurion (Tel Aviv); then train, bus or taxi to Ashkelon.
Dur.:	Full session (6 weeks) or half session (3 weeks); June to July.
Age:	Minimum 18, maximum 75 or older if fit.
Qualif.:	No previous experience necessary.
Work:	Work involves both the excavation of new material and the advanced curation of all material excavated since 1985. Current projects include the detailed analysis of Iron I pottery, Persian and Middle Bronze Age pottery alongside the ongoing registration and analysis of new finds. Volunteers are encouraged to learn about all parts of the archaeological process, including workshops about ground penetrating radar, flotation analysis, micromorphology, and other forms of scientific sampling.
Lang.:	English is necessary.
Accom.:	Full room & board at Ashkelon's finest, The Dan Gardens Hotel.
Cost:	US$2,900/full season; US$1,450/half season (including volunteer fees and hotel). College Credit available for an additional fee.
Applic.:	Deadline for registration April 15th. See website for details.

Louisbourg Archaeology Program

Fortress Louisbourg Association
265 Park Service Road
Louisbourg
Nova Scotia B1C 2L2 Canada
E-mail: folvol@auracom.com
www.fortressoflouisbourg.ca/archaeologyE/default.htm

Desc.: Archaeology enthusiasts can join supervised digs at the Fortress of Louisbourg National Historic Site of Canada. Current projects focus on field study at the De la Vallière property, which was occupied by French, British and New Englanders between 1720 and 1758. 10-12 participants/session take part in excavation, learn about archaeological field and lab techniques and attend presentations about current historical and archaeological research at the Fortress.

Per.: 18th-century French colonial fortress.

Country: Canada.

Loc.: Cape Breton Island, Nova Scotia.

Travel: Airplane/car to Halifax, Nova Scotia, then fly or drive to Sydney then half hour drive to Louisbourg. Visit website for details.

Dur.: 2, 5-day sessions; early-mid August.

Age: Minimum 18 (16 if accompanied by adult).

Qualif.: No experience necessary.

Work: Excavation, survey, artefact processing, field photography, daily presentations and tours of conservation labs, artefact and costume collections and siege sites. Ample opportunity for experiencing the Fortress Louisbourg and Cape Breton coastline.

Lang.: English, French.

Accom.: Various accommodation options in Louisbourg (see website).

Cost: CAD$650/5-day session; accommodation not included.

Applic.: Online form.

Notes: Non-excavation programmes with field and lab activities can be organised. Contact the Association for more information.

Lubbock Lake Landmark Regional Research Program

Museum of Texas Tech University
PO Box 43191 Lubbock, Texas USA
Tel.: ++1 (806) 742 2481 /742 1117 - Fax: ++1 (806) 742 1136
E-mail: eileen.johnson@ttu.edu
www.museum.ttu.edu/lll

Desc.:	Volunteers work with professional staff at the Lubbock Lake Landmark, Roland Springs Pleistocene fauna locality and post-archaeological survey testing and research programme. Lubbock Lake Landmark is a national historic and state archaeological landmark. Exhibits in the interpretive centre and guided tours of the excavation areas are open to the public.
Per.:	Clovis through Historic periods; 9500 BC to 1930 AD.
Country:	United States.
Loc.:	Lubbock, Texas.
Travel:	Transfer from Lubbock airport, about 20mi (30km), or bus station to the project is provided.
Dur.:	3- or 6-week sessions; June to August.
Age:	Minimum 18.
Qualif.:	No experience necessary.
Work:	Excavation, survey, geoarchaeological prospecting and mapping. Crew members help with daily kitchen and camp chores.
Lang.:	English.
Accom.:	Depending upon location, lodging is in 6-person tents, farm houses or trailers, with electricity and showers.
Cost:	No fees. Room & board included. Airfare, travel, tools, personal field supplies, insurance and personal expenses not included.
Applic.:	Contact the Project Director, Dr. Eileen Johnson. Academic credit available with approval from home university.
Notes:	Major equipment and field supplies provided; field kit available for US$40. Health and accident insurance and tetanus shot required.

Magura Uroiului Archaeological Project
The Museum of Dacian and Roman Civilisation in Deva
str. 1 Decembrie, 39 Deva 400123 Romania
Tel.: ++40 (254) 216 750 /(254) 212 200
Fax: ++40 (254) 212 200
Email: angelicabalos@yahoo.it; ardeu_adriana@yahoo.com
http://arheologie.worldwidesam.net/magura/

Desc.:	Excavations and fieldwalks have discovered Bronze Age, Hallstatt and La Tene (Dacian) settlements and earthwork fortifications, as well as a Roman villa and evidence of a Roman quarrying settlement. Minor attention has also been paid to the World War II anti-aircraft entrenchments and training trenches. The La Tene settlement and military trenches are located on plateaus at the base of the escarpment. The Roman villa is located to the side of the hill, and the Bronze and Iron Age earthwork fortifications are on the slope on the back of the hill. A Bronze Age and Neolithic settlement on top of the hill has not yet been excavated.
Per.:	Bronze and Iron Age, Roman.
Country:	Romania.
Loc.:	Magura Uroiului near Simeria, Romania.
Travel:	Details provided upon application.
Dur.:	3 weeks; August to September.
Age:	Minimum 18.
Qualif.:	No previous experience necessary.
Work:	Excavation, pratical training, cataloguing/drawing of finds, etc.
Lang.:	English.
Accom.:	Campsite near the excavation locations or possible billeting with a local family in the nearby village of Rapolt; 3 cooked meals/day.
Cost:	EUR150/week. Room & board, weekend excursions and local transportation included.
Applic.:	Project not running in 2009.

Maya Research Program

209 West Second Street No. 295
Fort Worth, Texas 76111 USA
Tel.: ++1 (817) 831 9011
E-mail: MRP@mrpmail.com
www.mayaresearchprogram.org

Desc.: The Program strives to understand the past and to inform the public about the Maya, preserve and protect Maya ruins and assist those with similar goals. For 17 years the Blue Creek Archaeological Project has studied the social, political and economic relationships that constituted ancient Maya society. MRP is a non-profit (501C-3) organization.

Per.: Classic Maya; 100-1200 AD.

Country: Belize.

Loc.: Blue Creek in north-western Belize.

Travel: Details provided upon application.

Dur.: 2-8 weeks; May to July.

Age: Minimum 18.

Qualif.: No experience necessary.

Work: Excavation, survey, laboratory work.

Lang.: English.

Accom.: Cabanas at base station.

Cost: US$1,450/2-week session (US$1,150 student discount); US$1,000 for each subsequent session. Room & board and project-related costs included. Transportation to and from Belize, airport departure tax and personal expenses not included.

Applic.: Online form.

Notes: The Harkrider Scholarship brings young US scholars to Latin America .

Middleborough Little League Site

Middleborough, MA 02346 USA
Bridgewater State College
Bridgewater MA 02325 USA
Tel.: ++1 (508) 531 2249
E-mail: c1hoffman@bridgew.edu
www.bridgew.edu

Desc.:	The programme is investigating a pre-European Native site where materials were being assembled for distribution to other regional sites for use in ceremonies.
Per.:	Early Archaic through Middle Woodland (8000-1000 BC).
Country:	United States.
Loc.:	Middleborough, Massachusetts.
Travel:	By car or commuter rail (1½ mi from station)
Dur.:	12 to 24 days; May 27th to July 1st.
Age:	Minimum 16.
Qualif.:	Prior fieldwork at Native sites in the Northeast; or register as a for-credit field school.
Work:	Excavation, survey, laboratory work.
Lang.:	English.
Accom.:	Dorm rooms at Bridgewater State College, about 8mi from site.
Cost:	US$738.15 tuition and fees per 12-day session for field school. Tools provided; no other project-related costs included. Personal expenses not included.
Applic.:	Online form at www.bridgew.edu/registrar (click on "Registration and Advising forms" to the left).
Notes:	Contact: Dr. Curtiss Hoffman, Anthropology Dept.

Midwest Archeological Center, National Park Service

Room 474, Federal Building
100 Centennial Mall North Lincoln, Nebraska 68508 USA
Tel.: ++1 (402) 437 5392 (ext. 114)
E-mail: Mark_Lynott@nps.gov; Dawn_Bringelson@nps.gov
www.nps.gov/mwac

Desc.:	The Midwest Archeological Center (MWAC) has an active, growing volunteer programme. The projects include the Cuyahoga Valley National Park in Ohio, Voyageurs National Park along the boundary waters in northern Minnesota, Wind Cave National Park in South Dakota and Fort Union Trading Post National Historic Site in North Dakota as well as assisting in the MWAC laboratory in the analysis of archaeological data from these and other projects. Please note: all projects pending passage of annual appropriations bills.
Per.:	Multi-period; early prehistoric to 19th and early 20th centuries.
Country:	United States.
Loc.:	Mainly within the Midwestern United States.
Travel:	It is the responsibility of the volunteer to get to MWAC or the work area at the beginning of their stay, and MWAC may be able to provide transport between the lodging and work site daily. This depends on project-specific conditions.
Dur.:	Minimum 1 week for field projects, lower intensity commitment in the lab; year round.
Age:	Minimum 18.
Qualif.:	No experience necessary.
Work:	Survey, inventory, excavation, lab inventory, cataloguing, analysis.
Lang.:	English.
Accom.:	Depending on each project's funding, MWAC may be able to provide housing at or near the project site. Type of housing and available funding varies by project.

Cost: Project-dependent. Volunteers may be reimbursed for out-of-pocket expenses (such as room & board) if funds are available.

Applic.: Online form. Individuals will be directed towards appropriate projects based upon their specified interests and available opportunities.

Notes: MWAC is always planning for new and ongoing projects. Interested parties should contact MWAC directly for information on specific project opportunities, or visit their website (above) to complete a volunteer application form. Non-US citizens or residents must also apply to the International Volunteers in Parks (IVIP) programme of the National Park Service. Consult the NPS Office of International Affairs webpage for information on the IVIP programme, application procedures and visa requirements (http://www.nps.gov/oia).

Montpelier Archaeological Expeditions

Montpelier Foundation
Montpelier Station, Virginia USA
Tel./Fax: ++1 (540) 672 2728 x160
E-mail: mreeves@montpelier.org
www.montpelier.org/explore/archaeology/excavation_programs.php

Desc.: An excavation of an early 19th-century detached kitchen and slave residence at James Madison's Montpelier located in Piedmont, Virginia, USA. Historical archaeology where volunteers will work with trained archaeology staff to uncover evidence for historic foundations, yard features, fencelines and historic artefacts (ceramics, glass, nails, personal items and bone).

Per.: 18th to 19th centuries.

Country: United States.

Loc.: Montpelier Station, Orange County, Virginia.

Travel: Train, bus or flight to Charlottesville; drive to Montpelier.

Dur.: 6 days; late March-mid May; August-early November.

Age: Minimum 16; maximum 75, or older if fit.

Qualif.: No previous experience necessary.

Work: Onsite training on use of instruments and tools, identification and retrieval of stratigraphic units (SU), examination and classification of artefacts (ceramics, glass, bone, iron, brick, mortar and stone), archaeological drawing, lab processing of soils and artefacts.

Lang.: English.

Accom.: Lodging in large antebellum home with full kitchen, laundry, sheets and towels provided. Board meals prepared by volunteers.

Cost: US$650. Accommodation included. Weekend excursions arranged for tours.

Applic.: See website for details.

The National Trust

Working Holidays Booking Office
Sapphire House, Roundtree Way, Norwich NR7 8SQ UK
Tel.: ++44 (844) 800 3099
Fax: ++44 (844) 800 8497
E-mail: working.holidays@nationaltrust.org.uk
www.nationaltrust.org.uk/volunteering

Desc.: The National Trust offers working holidays for non-professional individuals interested in an alternative vacation throughout the UK. The project may be an archaeological excavation, historical site preservation or drywall reconstruction.

Per.: Various.

Country: United Kingdom.

Loc.: England, Wales and Northern Ireland.

Travel: Details provided upon application.

Dur.: 1 week; year round.

Age: Minimum 18.

Qualif.: No technical skills required, but archaeological experience is welcomed.

Work: Digging and clearing. Workday is usually 9:00-17:00, weather permitting. Teamwork taking turns cooking and cleaning.

Lang.: English.

Accom.: Trust basecamp; farmhouse, cottage or apartment converted for group use. Most basecamps have a fully equipped kitchen, hot showers and bunk beds.

Cost: July to August: GB£100; other dates: GB£80. Travel and personal expenses not included. Supplementary GB£5/person for overseas bookings to cover UK bank and administrative charges.

Applic.: Online form or phone the Bookings Office at ++44 (844) 800 3099, stating the choice of holiday.

Notes: Work permits and visas are the responsibility of the volunteer. Bring a sleeping bag, raingear, work clothes, boots and gloves.

The Necropolis of the Roman City of Sanisera

Ecomuseum of the Cape of Cavalleria and the Sa Nitja Association
PO Box: APDO 68
07740 Es Mercadal, Menorca Spain
Tel./Fax: ++34 (971) 359 999 - Mob.: ++34 (608) 894 650
E-mail: sanisera@arrakis.es
www.ecomuseodecavalleria.com

Desc.:	The Ecomuseum is excavating of a cluster of Roman tombs from a cemetery located on the outskirts of the Roman city of Sanisera, appreciated for the quantity and quality of the amphorae and other Roman artefacts found (123 BC to 550 AD). Excavation led by Ecomuseum director Fernando Contreras in collaboration with physical anthropology and restoration specialists.
Per.:	Early Roman.
Country:	Spain.
Loc.:	Cape of Cavalleria, Es Mercadal, Menorca, Balearic Islands.
Travel:	Details provided upon application.
Dur.:	8 sessions, 20 days each; May to October.
Age:	Minimum 18.
Work:	7hrs/day, divided between excavation of the tombs and lab work studying and conserving recovered materials. Lectures on methodology, Roman archaeology, physical anthropology and conservation of archaeological materials. Field trips organised to other archaeological sites on the island. 2 days off/8 course days.
Lang.:	English and Spanish.
Accom.:	Student residency (air-conditioned), in town of Ciutadella within walking distance of the historic centre, port and beaches.
Cost:	US$1,800-2,300; room & board, transportation to and from the excavation site, organised excursions, travel/medical insurance, application fee and administrative cost included. Travel expenses not included. Costs subject to change.
Applic.:	E-mail or online with US$200 deposit. Balance due 30 days before start. See also: Underwater Archaeology in the Mediterranean Sea.

Nent Valley Archaeological Research Project

Nenthead Mines Heritage Centre / Nenthead Research Project
Dilston Castle, Nenthead
Cumbria CA9 3PD UK
Tel./Fax: ++44 (1434) 382 045 /(1434) 382 043
E-mail:fieldschool@nparchaeology.co.uk
www.nparchaeology.co.uk

Desc.: This project is divided between the research of one of Britain's most significant lead mining sites and Dilston Castle, which was occupied from the 13th century to the late 18th century. Both sites are well established and have produced superb archaeological remains during the last 7 years of fieldwork.

Per.: 13th to 20th centuries and previous periods.

Country: United Kingdom.

Loc.: Dilston Castle, Corbridge, Northumberland, UK.

Travel: Train to Corbridge, then pick-up to site on Monday mornings.

Dur.: 8 weeks; June to July.

Age: Minimum 16; maximum 75, or older if fit.

Qualif.: No previous experience necessary.

Work: On-site training covers all aspects of archaeological fieldwork including: excavation techniques, archaeological planning techniques, environmental and finds processing techniques, building recording techniques, computer aided drawing (digitising), geophysical surveying techniques.

Lang.: English.

Accom.: Lodging in bunkhouse with hot water showers and self-catering cooking facilities.

Cost: US£125/week, accommodation included.

Applic.: Deadline for registration June 6th. See website for details.

Newbarns Project
Stewartry Archaeological Trust

Kingston, Rhonehouse, Castle Douglas
Kirkcudbrightshire, Scotland DG7 1SA UK
Tel. ++44 (1556) 680 478
E-mail: lizzie@sjcresearch.co.uk
www.sat.org.uk

Desc.:	Newbarns Project regards 3 pre-historic kerb cairns with inhumation and cremation burials. It presents later settlement evidence, Iron Age and Medieval.
Per.:	3000 BC to 1500 AD.
Country:	Scotland.
Loc.:	Colvend Parish, Dumfries and Galloway.
Travel:	Train, coach, car. Travel is volunteer's responsibility.
Dur.:	July to September.
Age:	Minimum 17; maximum 75, or older if fit.
Qualif.:	No previous experience necessary.
Work:	On-site training covers the correct use of instruments and tools, identification, examination and classification of finds (pottery, metalwork), archaeological drawing, survey, plane tabling.
Lang.:	English.
Accom.:	Diggers provide their own accommodation; numerous caravan, camp sites and B&Bs are available locally. .
Cost:	US£35/week towards dig expenses.
Applic.:	Deadline for registration May 31st. See website for details.

NICE — Never-ending International WorkCamps Exchange

2-1-14-401 Shinjuku, Shinjuku-ku
Tokyo 160-0022 Japan
Tel.: ++81 (3) 3358 7140 - Fax: ++81 (3) 3358 7149
E-mail: nice@nice1.gr.jp
http://nice1.gr.jp

Desc.: Cultural exchanges and workcamps in various sectors including culture and renovation. There are workcamps aimed at maintaining the local cultural heritage of a Japanese traditional house. One location is in Tonami, an area famous for beautiful scenery of the scattered houses and the local cultural heritage of the traditional Japanese reed-roofed houses; the other is in Yawata, among the most productive areas for rice and known for its snowy winters.

Per.: Various.

Country: Japan and East Asia. Projects abroad available for Japanese citizens.

Dur.: Usually 3 weeks; year round.

Age: Minimum 18.

Qualif.: No experience necessary.

Work: May include cutting and carrying reeds for the roofs and assisting the carpenters. 6-8 hrs/day; Monday to Friday.

Lang.: English, Japanese.

Accom.: Basic facilities or tent camping.

Cost: Fees paid to sending workcamp organisation. Additional fees (US$100-200) in some workcamps may be required. Room & board and project support included. A membership fee covers monthly newsletters and insurance.

Applic.: Japanese volunteers may apply directly. Foreign volunteers must apply to a partner workcamp organisation of home country; see the Alliance of European Voluntary Service Organizations or the Coordinating Committee for International Voluntary Service at UNESCO in Paris.

North East Hants Historical & Archaeological Society

2 Rotherwick Court, Alexandra Road
Farnborough, GU14 6DD UK
Tel.: ++44 (1252) 548 115
E-mail: nehhas@hantsweb.org.uk
www.hants.org.uk/nehhas

Desc.: The project focuses on a Roman road from Winchester to London. Surveys and excavations on Bank Holiday are during weekends from Easter to August.

Per.: 50-400AD.

Country: England.

Loc.: Hampshire.

Travel: Flight to Gatwick or Heathrow.

Dur.: Surveys on weekends, excavations on Bank Holiday weekends, from Easter to August, 4 days each.

Age: Minimum 16, younger if accompanied by an adult.

Qualif.: No experience necessary.

Work: Excavation, survey, post-excavation work.

Lang.: English.

Accom.: Leads and campsites provided.

Cost: GB£10 membership, GB£60 for training. Airport departure tax and personal expenses not included.

Applic.: Online form at www.hants.org.uk/nehhas.

North Pennines Heritage Trust

Nenthead Mines Visitor Centre
Nenthead, Alston, Cumbria CA93PD UK
Tel.: ++44 (1434) 382 037 /382 045
Fax: ++44 (1434) 382 294
E-mail: fieldschool@nparchaeology.co.uk
www.nparchaeology.co.uk

Desc.: Volunteers can take part in a variety of fieldwork projects including the Diston Castle excavation and a series of smaller research excavations at Nenthead Mines. Work ranges from field survey and building recording to fieldwork and post-excavation work. There are also opportunities in archive and research projects.

Per.: 12th to 19th centuries.

Country: United Kingdom.

Loc.: Nenthead, Cumbria.

Travel: Volunteers are responsible for their transportation to the Trust.

Dur.: 2 weeks; June and July.

Age: Minimum 17.

Qualif.: No experience necessary.

Work: Survey, excavation, restoration, post-excavation, archiving and research.

Lang.: English.

Accom.: Self-catering accommodation provided at the Trust bunkhouse with a kitchen, bathroom, lounge area and washroom.

Cost: GB£125/week, includes accommodation at Trust bunkhouse and fieldschool fees.

Applic.: All details are on the field school section of the website including online booking form.

Noviodunum Archaeological Project

University College London
31-34 Gordon Square
London WC1H 0PY UK
Tel.: ++44 (20) 7679 7495
E-mail: noviodunum@hotmail.com
http://www.ucl.ac.uk/archaeology/project/noviodunum/index.htm

Desc.: For several years, Noviodunum Archaeological Project has been investigating an important Roman and Byzantine naval base and town, as well as sites in the hinterland. Surveys have revealed Late Roman walls and a structure that could be a granary. In the upcoming seasons the project will explore the underlying settlement in an adjacent area used as a cemetery during the Medieval period.

Per.: Roman period.

Country: Romania.

Loc.: Isaccea, eastern Romania

Travel: Flight to Bucharest; further details upon application.

Dur.: 3-6 weeks; July to August.

Age: Minimum 18.

Qualif.: No previous experience necessary.

Work: Excavation, finds processing, recording and drawing; environmental and finds work. All necessary training will be given. 5-6 days/week.

Lang.: English.

Accom.: Basic ammenities in a local school in Isaccea. Food provided (vegetarian diets can be arranged).

Cost: GB£400/3 weeks, GB£600/6-week excavation season. Transfer from Bucharest to Isaccea, local transport, room and board are included.

Nuvuk Archaeology Project Excavation

Barrow Arctic Science Consortium
Barrow, AK 99723 USA
Tel. ++1 (907) 852 3050
E-mail: anne.jensen@uicscience.org

Desc.: The village of Nuvuk was once located at the tip of Point Barrow, Alaska. A survey has revealed many ancient unmarked graves, an Ipiutak campsite, contact-era work areas and apparent tent sites in severe danger of erosion. This is the largest known Thule/Iñupiat cemetery from North Alaska, perhaps anywhere in the Arctic. Students excavate threatened cultural resources and save the data about the past 1,600 or 1,700 years of history. Much of the field crew are local North Slope high school students.

Per.: Ipiutak, Thule, Pre-contact to Recent Iñupiat.

Country: United States.

Loc.: Point Barrow, Alaska.

Travel: Details provided upon application.

Dur.: Minimum 2 weeks, maximum 5 weeks; June and July.

Age: Minimum 18.

Qualif.: Qualified students and non-credit volunteers interested in the archaeology and culture of the Alaskan North Slope.

Work: Survey, excavation, mapping, material processing, record keeping.

Lang.: English.

Accom.: Rented houses, north of Barrow, with shared bathroom and kitchen facilities. A cafeteria is nearby. Lunch provided in field.

Cost: Volunteers US$5,520; students US$6,190 (with course registration and tuition through Ilisagvik College). Room & board, project travel to Barrow and fees included. Travel and personal expenses not included. Costs subject to change.

Applic.: Via e-mail. Applications due March 30th.

Ometepe Petroglyph Project

Culturelink
609 Aileen Street, Oakland
California 94609 USA
Tel./Fax: ++1 (510) 654 8635
E-mail: suzannebaker@earthlink.net
www.culturelink.info

Desc.: A volunteer archaeological field survey along the northern slopes of the Maderas volcano, the eastern half of Ometepe Island, Nicaragua. Almost 1700 petroglyph panels on 1400 boulders have been photographed, drawn and catalogued as part of the survey. Isla Ometepe is relatively rich in pre-Columbian sites, artefacts and a monumental sculptural tradition and to contain numerous petroglyphs, which are being systematically recorded.

Per.: Dinarte phase, early Polychrome (ca. 2000-500 BC) to Spanish contact (ca. 1522 AD).

Country: Nicaragua.

Loc.: Ometepe Island, the largest island on Lake Nicaragua.

Travel: Meet at the International Airport in Managua. Bus and boat to the Island, then on to the town of Balgües near the project location.

Dur.: 2 weeks to 1 month; dry season, January, February or March.

Age: Minimum 18.

Qualif.: No experience necessary, but survey experience preferred.

Work: Field walking, survey, mapping, drawing and photographing the petroglyphs, collecting and washing diagnostic pottery, inking maps and drawings, cataloguing and archiving data.

Lang.: English, Spanish.

Accom.: Old hacienda building on a coffee cooperative. Dorm-style rooms, basic showers and plumbing.

Cost: US$450/week. In-country transport, accommodation and basic meals included. Consult website for further details.

Applic.: See website for details.

PaleoWorld Research Foundation Expeditions

PO Box 5080, Englewood
Florida 34224 USA
Tel./Fax: ++1 (941) 473 9511
E-mail: paleoworld@paleoworld.org
www.paleoworld.org

Desc: The Foundation provides a unique 100% hands-on educational opportunity to participate and explore the science of dinosaur palaeontology. China expeditions are also available through the Sinofossa Institute in Beijing, China. Families are welcome.

Per.:   Paleonthology.

Country: United States.

Loc.:   North-eastern Montana, in the town of Jordan; the field expedition is within 21mi (55km) of the town, on private land.

Travel: Flight to Logan, Billings, Montana. Rental car available.

Dur.:   Dig-for-a-Day or stay the summer; June to August.

Age: Minimum 18, unless with parents for a family dig.

Qualif.:   No experience necessary.

Work: Survey, excavation, fossil preparation (plaster jacketing, casting and moulding) and removal and quarry mapping. Hiking, digging and hauling within limits.

Lang.:   English.

Accom.:   There are 2 motels and several restaurants in town. It is possible to join the PWRF research team at basecamp: meals, toilet/shower and laundry facilities available in several mobile homes and campers. RV and tent campsites also available.

Cost: US$125/day for adults, US$65/day for children 15yrs and under. Meal and lodging plans available. Students working on a palaeontology related degree only charged room & board.

Applic.:   Registration, medical and liability forms must be filled in and submitted along with a non-refundable deposit.

Pambamarca Archaeological Project

UCLA Archaeology Field Program
International Education Office B300 Murphy Hall
Los Angeles, CA 90095 USA
Tel. ++1 (310) 825 4995
E-mail: ieo@international.ucla.edu
www.pambamarca.net

Desc.: This project investigates the largest concentration of Pre-Columbian forts in the New World. The ancient fortresses of Pambamarca speak of a significant moment in Andean prehistory when the Incan Empire's expansion was brought to a standstill by the fierce and effective local resistance. Participants study the identity of these resisters and how the Incas managed to finally overcome them. The focus of investigations will include pre-Inca settlements, the design and construction of the fortresses themselves and the road network that leads into and out of the region. Additionally, participants have the opportunity to conduct an independent research project aimed at connecting the ancient remains with historic and living landscapes in order to construct a complete picture of life in and around Pambamarca.

Per.: Inca and Pre-Inca 1400-1550 AD.

Country: Ecuador.

Loc.: Cayambe.

Travel: Plane to Quito (UIO), meeting at airport.

Dur.: 4 weeks; June and July

Age: 18 or older.

Qualif.: No previous experience necessary.

Work: Excavation, survey and exploration of ancient road systems and use of Ground Penetrating Radar (GPR) to detect subsurface features and Geographic Information System (GIS) to analyze data; training in archaeological field techniques, mapping, field excavation and laboratory analysis provided.

Lang.: English and Spanish.

Accom.: Haicenda Guachala (www.guachala.com) or in the town of Cangahua; accommodation varies with project focus – see www.pambamarca.net.

Cost: US$4000. Non-UCLA participant must add US$1500 for room & board plus tuition costs. International airfare not included.

Applic.: Registration deadline in April for UCLA and June for Foothill College. See website for details. www.pambamarca.net.

Passport in Time

Passport in Time Clearinghouse
PO Box 15728, Rio Rancho, New Mexico USA
Tel.: ++1 (800) 281 9176 (toll free) /(505) 896 1136
Fax: ++1 (505) 896 1136
E-mail: volunteer@passportintime.com
www.passportintime.com

Desc.:	Passport in Time is a volunteer archaeology and historic preservation programme of the US Forest Service. Volunteers work with professional archaeologists on activities such as archaeological excavation or survey, restoration of historic structures and cataloguing historic photographs. Past projects have included preservation of ancient cliff dwellings in New Mexico, excavation of a 19th-century Chinese mining site in Hell's Canyon, Idaho, restoration of a turn-of-the-20th century log cabin in Montana and documentation of ancient rock art in Colorado.
Per.:	Various.
Country:	United States.
Loc.:	Various.
Travel:	Depends on project, inquire for details.
Dur.:	Various. Most projects are 5 days; year round.
Age:	Minimum 18.
Qualif.:	No experience necessary.
Work:	Field or office. Examples: excavation, survey, archival research, historic structure restoration, gathering oral histories.
Lang.:	English.
Accom.:	Varies with project, including backcountry camping with personal gear, campsites with hook-ups for RVs or local hotels. Some projects offer meals prepared by a camp cook, often for a small fee.
Cost:	No fee to participate. Travel not included.
Applic.:	Online form.
Notes:	Volunteers with disabilities accepted when and wherever possible.

Pella Volunteer Scheme

University of Sydney
NEAF, SOPHI A14, NSW 2006 Australia
Tel.: ++61 (2) 9351 4151 - Fax: ++61 (2) 9552 1412
E-mail: neaf@antiquity.usyd.edu.au
www.arts.usyd.edu.au/foundations/neaf/

Desc.:	The research focuses on the Bronze Age Migdol Temple, as well as on the temple outbuildings, a Middle Bronze Age gate and Late Roman storehouses. The major ruin field at Pella covers an area of 10ha, although recent work by the Pella Hinterland Survey shows that the landscape was scattered with farmsteads, industrial installations and burials beyond the main areas of settlement.
Per.:	Bronze Age to Late Roman.
Country:	Jordan.
Loc.:	Pella.
Travel:	Details provided upon application.
Dur.:	3 weeks; January and February.
Age:	Minimum 18.
Qualif.:	No experience or professional qualifications necessary.
Work:	Excavation, sampling and bagging artefacts. Part-time digging and working in the trenches and cleaning, sorting and identifying artefacts. Training provided.
Lang.:	English.
Accom.:	Pella dig house, located in a compound on the main tell, with shared rooms (couples are accepted); all bedding provided; hot and cold running water, western-style bathing facilities; laundry; and mix of Arabic and Western food is provided.
Cost:	AUS$3,500 (approximatelyUS$2,285), subject to currency fluctuations. Transfers to and from the dig and full room and board included. Airfare not included.
Applic.:	Online form.

Piddington

Upper Nene Archaeological Society (UNAS)
Toadhall, 86 Main Road, Hackleton, Northampton NN7 2AD UK
Tel.: ++44 (1604) 870 312 - Fax: ++44 (1604) 871 266
E-mail: piddington.museum@tiscali.co.uk;
unas@friendship-taylor.freeserve.co.uk
www.unas.org.uk; www.members.aol.com

Desc.:	The Upper Nene Archaeological Society was formed in 1962 by several active local fieldworkers who wanted to share their knowledge about the area's prehistoric and Roman past. An independent society and a registered charity, UNAS aims to promote study and interest in archaeology, the discovery and investigation of sites and the preservation of items of archaeological interest of all periods. The Piddington project is an excavation of a Late Iron Age settlement and Romano-British villa.
Per.:	Late Iron Age and Romano-British.
Country:	United Kingdom.
Loc.:	Piddington off B526 Northampton-Newport Pagnell Road.
Travel:	Train from London Euston to Northampton.
Dur.:	4 weeks; August.
Age:	Minimum 18. Special consideration may be given to very keen 15-17-year-old volunteers.
Qualif.:	No experience necessary.
Work:	Excavation.
Lang.:	English.
Accom.:	Limited accommodation can be arranged. Camping next to the site. Meals arranged.
Cost:	GB£38/3 weeks for members; GB£45 for non-members; GB£30 and GB£35 respectively for 2 weeks; GB£20/week for members only. Costs subject to change.
Applic.:	Include a self-addressed envelope or 2 IRCs with application.
Notes:	Contact Roy or Liz Friendship-Taylor.

Poulton Research Project

17 Canadian Avenue, Chester CH2 3HG UK
Tel.: ++44 (1244) 318 200
E-mail: c.caroe@btinternet.com
www.poultonproject.org

Desc.: This is a long-term research investigation into the evolution of the historic, environmental, social and economic landscape of Cheshire, in particular the hinterland of Chester. It is based on a Medieval chapel associated with the lost Cistercian Abbey of Poulton together with its associated cemetery. The site has also provided positive locational evidence for a Roman villa/farmstead/temple. The excavation of a second Bronze Age Ring ditch and massive enclosure ditch has been also undertaken. The Project is community based and welcomes volunteers and students as well as special needs groups.

Per.: Multi-period; Neolithic to 20th century.

Country: United Kingdom.

Loc.: 5mi (8km) south of Chester, on the Welsh border.

Travel: Flight to Manchester or Liverpool or train, bus or car to Chester. Transport to/from site can be provided; see website for location.

Dur.: Easter and June to September. See website for details.

Age: Minimum 16. No maximum if physically fit for hard labour.

Qualif.: No experience necessary. Mainly university students.

Work: Excavation.

Lang.: English.

Accom.: None provided. Campsite or hostel nearby.

Cost: GB£100/week or GB£20/day.

Applic.: Online form to send via e-mail.

Notes: Contact Chris Caroe.

Pre-Roman Culture in the Province of Zamora Project

Proyecto de Investigación y Difusión del Patrimonio Arqueológico
Protohistórico de la provincia de Zamora (P.I.D.P.A.P.Z.)
C/ Camarena 292, 2D 28047 Madrid Spain
E-mail: zamoraprotohistorica@gmail.com
http://zamoraprotohistorica.blogspot.com

Desc.:	The research focuses on the pre-Roman settlement in the Spanish north-western region of Zamora. The main features of the project are the studies of defensive systems, environmental relationship, rock art, Iron Age pottery and later Roman metalworking.
Per.:	Late Bronze Age to Iron Age Romanization.
Country:	Spain.
Loc.:	Peñas de la Cerca - El Castillon sites (Zamora, NW Spain).
Travel:	Airplane to Madrid then bus to Zamora where volunteers are met by project leaders.
Dur.:	6 weeks; July and August.
Age:	Minimum 18.
Qualif.:	No experience necessary.
Work:	Excavation, survey, laboratory work.
Lang.:	Spanish, and English when available.
Accom.:	Base station in Puebla de Sanabria and Tabara.
Cost:	Room & board and project-related costs included. Travel to Madrid and transportation to the site not included.
Applic.:	Online form.
Notes:	Tourist visits around north-western Spain are offered free.

Projects Abroad

Aldsworth Parade, Goring by sea
Sussex UK
Tel.: ++44 (1903) 708 300
Fax: ++44 (1903) 708 309
E-mail: info@projects-abroad.co.uk
www.projects-abroad.co.uk

Desc.: Rediscover ancient cultures at the archaeology programme in Romania and the Inca Projects programme in Peru. In Peru, volunteers work in the historic town of Huyro. In Romania, volunteers work with the National Museum of History to investigate ancient Dacia and the Medieval principality of Transylvania.

Per.: Inca in Peru; Iron Age in Romania.

Country: Peru, Romania.

Loc.: Huyro in the Andes; Dacia, Brasov county, in the Carpathians.

Travel: Details provided upon application.

Dur.: Typically 1, 2 or 3 months. Duration is volunteer's choice.

Age: Minimum17; maximum 70.

Qualif.: No experience necessary.

Work: Physical work similar to dry stonewalling to reconstruct the Inca terraces and the canals of the Sacred Valley in Peru; excavation in Romania with potential museum work.

Lang.: English. In Peru good spoken Spanish is necessary.

Accom.: Local host families, hostels or other types of accommodation.

Cost: GB£2,295 for Romania and Peru; for programmes up to 3 months. A deposit of GB£195 is required with the application. Room & board, insurance and staff support included. International travel not included.

Applic.: Online form. Receipt of application, deposit payment and formal letter of acceptance will be sent within 15 working days. Apply at least 2 months in advance to allow time for visa and travel arrangements.

The Ramat Rahel Archaeological Project

Tel Aviv University (Israel) and Heidelberg Universität (Germany)
Kibbutz Ramat Rachel Jerusalem 90900 Israel
E-mail: omertelaviv@gmail.com
www.tau.ac.il/~rmtrachl/the_site.html
www.ramatrachel.co.il/ARCHEOLOGY/VolunteerPrograms.htm

Desc.:	Seated high above the modern city of Jerusalem is the ancient site of Ramat Rahel. Excavation continues to uncover the stories of a palatial centre and garden built at the time of the kings of Judah and during the return from exile; a Jewish community from the days of the Second Temple until its destruction in the great rebellion (ca. 70 BC); and a Christian monastery and church built halfway between the 2 holy cities of Jerusalem and Bethlehem.
Per.:	Iron Age to Abbasside period; 7th century BC to 10th century AD.
Country:	Israel.
Loc.:	Kibbutz Ramat Rahel, Jerusalem.
Travel:	From Tel Aviv airport (TLV) to Jerusalem (see programs website).
Dur.:	Minimum 7 days;.mid-July to mid-August.
Age:	Minimum 16; maximum 99.
Qualif.:	No previous experience necessary.
Work:	On-site training: use of instruments and tools; identification and retrieval of stratigraphic units (SU); examination and classification of finds (pottery, numismatics, glass fragments, anthropology); archaeological drawing, survey and graphical reconstruction.
Lang.:	English.
Accom.:	4-star Ramat Rahel Hotel; room & board, internet/office services, academic lectures, evening tours to the holy city of Jerusalem and weekend tours to historical sites all over Israel included.
Cost:	See website at: http://www.tau.ac.il/~rmtrachl/the_site.html.
Applic.:	Deadline for registration June 1st. For more information see http://www.tau.ac.il/~rmtrachl/the_site.html.

Rock Art Documentation and Education Project

African Conservation Trust
PO Box 310 Link Hills 3652 South Africa
Tel.: ++27 (31) 767 5044
Fax: ++27 (86) 511 7594
E-mail: info@projectafrica.com
www. projectafrica.com

Desc.: The Ukhahlamba Drakensberg Park (UDP) is internationally regarded as among the finest resources for rock art. There are an estimated 40,000 paintings at some 550 sites in the Drakensberg, dating back thousands of years. The history is well documented but inaccessible to many. Sensitive heritage material needs to be documented and protected to ensure a record remains intact.

Per.: Multi-period; early Medieval to modern.

Country: South Africa.

Loc.: Ukhahlamba Drakensberg National Park, KwaZulu-Natal, near the border with Lesotho.

Travel: Meeting and pick-up at Durban International Airport (DUR).

Dur.: 4 weeks; arrivial and departure dates flexible. Inquire for details.

Age: Minimum 17.

Qualif.: No experience necessary.

Work: Build shepherds huts with the local community so that mountain shepherds no longer have to use shelters containing rock art. Assist with erosion gully rehabilitation works and development of eco-tourism initiatives in the area.

Lang.: English.

Accom.: Camping. Bring tent and personal camping equipment.

Cost: GB£950/4 weeks; airfare not included.

Applic.: Online form.

Roman Fort on Tyne

Earthwatch Institute
Mayfield House, 256 Banbury Road,
Oxford OX2 7DE UK
Tel.: ++44 (1865) 318 831 - Fax: ++44 (1865) 311 383
E-mail: info@earthwatch.org.uk
www.earthwatch.org/europe

Desc.: A couple millennia ago, the Roman Empire stretched to northern England, where the Romans considered the edge of civilization. Arbeia, the Roman fort overlooking the river and harbour from Lawe Top, became part of one of the largest and busiest supply depots in the area as it was less than 4mi (6.5km) from Hadrian's Wall. The Empire built the wall to mark its northern boundary and protect its settlements from the region's native inhabitants such as the Brigantes and Picts. How these cultures adapted to each other and coexisted have intriguing parallels throughout world history and may hold important lessons for today's cultures.

Per.: Pre-Roman Iron Age to Late Roman.

Country: United Kingdom.

Loc.: South Shields, England.

Travel: Contact the organisation for details.

Dur.: 14 days, June. There is also a team for teenagers in July.

Age: Minimum 18. Teen team exclusively for 16 and 17 year olds.

Qualif.: No special skills or experience required.

Work: Volunteers work in groups of 4-5, rotating among many tasks: stratigraphic excavation, recording site data, site surveying, sampling, cleaning, processing finds.

Lang.: English.

Accom.: Local guesthouses with shared bedrooms and hot water; walking distances to the site as well as to parks, beaches, restaurants.

Cost: GB£1,435.

Applic.: Telephone or e-mail for instructions.

"Roman Project" Archaeological Program

Bulgarian Archaeological Association
21 Tsarigradsko shosse Blv.
1124 Sofia Bulgaria
Tel.: ++359 (878) 680 524
E-mail: info@archbg.net
www.archaeology.archbg.net

Desc.:	The Bulgarian Archaeological Association offers volunteers the opportunity to excavate at 3 different archaeological sites in the region, all with extensive Roman-era remains. Volunteers can help uncover the ruins of a massive Roman fortress with outer walls still standing to a height of over 20ft. Overlooking the banks of the Archar River in Aniste, volunteers can help excavate an expansive ancient villa and bath and, at Conbustica, one of the largest Roman towns of the lower Danube.
Per.:	Roman and Late Antique Ages; 1st to 6th centuries AD.
Country:	Bulgaria.
Loc.:	North-western Bulgaria, towns of Belogradchik and Vidin.
Travel:	Flight to Sofia (SOF), then bus to Belogradchik where volunteers are met by project leaders.
Dur.:	2-4 weeks; July to September.
Age:	Minimum 16.
Qualif.:	No experience necessary.
Work:	Excavation, survey, laboratory work.
Lang.:	English.
Accom.:	Hotel in the city centre.
Cost:	EUR1,248/2-week session. Different modules available. Room & board and project-related costs included. Transportation to and from Belize, airport departure tax and personal expenses not included.
Applic.:	Online form.

Romans in the Mediterranean Islands: The City of Sanisera

Ecomuseum of the Cape of Cavalleria and the Sa Nitja Association
PO Box: APDO 68, 07740 Es Mercadal, Menorca Spain
Tel./Fax: ++34 (971) 359 999 - Mob.: ++34 (608) 894 650
E-mail: sanisera@arrakis.es
www.ecomuseodecavalleria.com

Desc.: The project is excavating the Roman City of Sanisera, that overlooks the natural port of Sanitja. The Romans first arrived on Menorca in the year 123 BC when the Roman army conquered the Balearic Islands. For 600 years more, Menorca would form a part of the immense Roman Empire. On the island, the Romans formed 3 cities. Of those cities, Sanisera was built around the port of Sanitja in the most northern part of the island. The city flourished due to the heavy maritime commercial industry that received boats going from Spain to Italy and from France to Africa. The impressiveness of Sanisera can be appreciated in the present by the quantity and quality of the amphoras and other roman artifacts that have been found in recent excavations. Sanisera is situated in the spectacular natural reserve next to the Ecomuseum of the Cape of Cavalleria.

Per.: Early Roman.

Country: Spain.

Loc.: Cape of Cavalleria, Es Mercadal, Menorca, the Balearic Islands.

Travel: Details provided upon application.

Dur.: 8 sessions, 20 days each; May to October.

Age: Minimum 18.

Work: Students will learn and gain experience in excavation using the Harris Matrix. Various instruments and tools will be used to record stratigraphy and document the plans and photographs of the excavation. In the museum laboratory, students will process excavated material and will be trained in the basic techniques of artifact recording, focusing on roman pottery, such as amphora. The course runs 7hrs/day which is divided between excavation and laboratory work, studying and conservation of the materials recovered. In addition, students will also participate in conferences on methodology and roman archaeology, and will visit other museums and archaeological sites on the island. For every 8 course days there are 2 days off.

Lang.: English and Spanish

Accom.: Participants will stay in the Ecomuseum's student residency in Ciutadella (air-conditioned), within walking distance of the historic center, port, and beaches. Ciutadella is an enchanting Mediterranean town, lively with cafés and outdoor terraces hidden among narrow cobble stone streets. Transportation to and from the excavation site and planned excursions are included.

Cost: US$1,800-2,100, including full room and board, transportation, accidental medical insurance, planned excursions, application fee and administrative cost. Airfare not included. Costs are subject to change.

Applic.: Via e-mail or online application form. US$200 deposit plus final payment due 30 days before the start of the elected session.

Rushen Abbey Field School

University of Liverpool, Centre for Manx Studies
6 Kingswood Grove, Douglas
Isle of Man, IM1 3LX UK
Tel.: ++44 (1624) 695 160 - Fax: ++44 (1624) 678 752
E-mail: rushenabbeydig@manx.net
www.liv.ac.uk/manxstudies/rushen/field_school.htm

Desc.: Founded in 1134, the Abbey was originally home for monks of the Savignac order but soon came under Cistercian control and remained so until its dissolution. The abbey is located 2mi (3km) from Castle Rushen, the most important political entity on the island in Medieval times. Since 1998 Liverpool University and The Centre for Manx Studies have conducted a research programme and excavations to better understand the nature of this fascinating archaeological site.

Per.: Medieval.

Country: Isle of Man.

Loc.: Ballasalla, southern Isle of Man.

Travel: Details provided upon application.

Dur.: 2 weeks for field school; June and July.

Age: Minimum 18.

Qualif.: No previous experience necessary.

Work: Excavation, recording, drawing, finds processing, etc.

Lang.: English.

Accom.: Not included. Volunteers provide own lodging and transport.

Cost: Free of charge. GB£105 tuition for 2 week field school.

Applic.: Online form.

La Sabranenque

Rue de la Tour de l'Oume
30290 Saint Victor la Coste France
Tel.: ++33 (4) 6650 0505
Fax: ++33 (4) 6650 1248
E-mail: info@sabranenque.com
www.sabranenque.com

Desc.: Summer Volunteer sessions allow volunteers to join with La Sabranenque to take part in the on-going restoration of Mediterranean architecture projects. Volunteer & Visit is a work programme on historic sites coupled with outings that offer the discovery of the towns, monuments and countryside of Provence.

Per.: Medieval to 19th century.

Country: France, Italy.

Loc.: Various villages.

Travel: Details provided upon application.

Dur.: 2 weeks; June to September for Summer Volunteer sessions. 1 week; May to October for Volunteer & Visit.

Age: Minimum 18.

Qualif.: No experience necessary.

Work: Variable, but most involve stone masonry. Other techniques used include any stage of historic restoration, from clearing rubble to roof tiling, stone cutting, flooring with tiles or wood, interior plastering, arch and vault construction, path paving, dry-stone walling, etc. Mornings and occasionally afternoons.

Lang.: English, French or Italian.

Accom.: Stone houses in the old village that La Sabranenque has restored; double occupancy.

Cost: Inquiry for current participation fee. Room, board and project-related expenses included.

Applic.: Online form.

Saveock Water Archaeology

Saveock Mill, Greenbottom,
Truro, Cornwall TR4 8QQ UK
Tel.: ++44 (1872) 560 351
E-mail: jacqui@archaeologyonline.org
www.archaeologyonline.org

Desc.:	Saveock Water Archaeology has had considerable international media interest in it owing to its seemingly unique pagan swanfeather pits. Underlying the pits are the remains of a Hunter Gatherer settlement followed by Neolithic and Bronze Age features. This is a permanent archaeology centre so full indoor facilities during wet weather have been provided. Lecture given each week by world renowned Site Director Jacqui Wood on Experimental Archaeology.
Per.:	Mesolithic 8000 BC to 17th-century Pagan deposits.
Country:	Great Britain.
Loc.:	4mi (6-7km) from Truro, Cornwall, south-western Britain.
Travel:	Details provided upon application.
Dur.:	Minimum 5 days; April to August.
Age:	Minimum 14 if accompanied by adult. Minimum 17 if alone.
Qualif.:	Saveock welcomes all from university students to keen amateurs. The only qualification is enthusiasm to discover the past.
Work:	Excavation, planning, section drawing, context sheets, finds processing, wet-sieving data recording, conservation, etc. 10:00-16:00, Monday to Friday.
Lang.:	English.
Accom.:	Accommodation not included, but a list of local accommodation including campsites or guest houses available.
Cost:	GB£185/5days, equipment, lunch and refreshments included.
Applic.:	Send booking form mail with GB£185 by cheque in sterling.

SCI — Service Civil International

International Secretariat
St. Jacobsmarkt 82, B-2000 Antwerpen Belgium
Tel.: ++32 (3) 226 5727
Fax: ++32 (3) 232 0344
E-mail: info@sciint.org
www.sciint.org

Desc.:	SCI is a voluntary NGO founded in 1920 to promote international understanding and peace. It provides volunteers for projects worldwide for communities that cannot afford labour. Every year more than 20,000 international volunteers work in over 100 camps. There are 33 international branches organised in national working groups, local groups and a national committee.
Per.:	Various.
Country:	Worldwide.
Loc.:	Various.
Travel:	Details provided upon application to specific project.
Dur.:	2-3 weeks; mainly June to September. People with workcamp experience can volunteer for 3-6 months.
Age:	Minimum 18 for Europe; minimum 16 for North America.
Qualif.:	No experience necessary.
Work:	Reconstruction of cultural and historical buildings; workcamps.
Lang.:	English. For other languages, inquire with local SCI office.
Accom:	Typically tent camping or dormitories. Bring a sleeping bag.
Cost:	See local branches websites for detailed costs.
Applic.:	Standard application; no need to be a member. Contact the nearest national branch for information.
Notes:	SCI Germany: www.sci-d.de; SCI-IVS USA: www.sci-ivs.org; IVS (International Voluntary Service part of a wider international group in the British chapter of SCI): www.ivsgb.org; IVP Australia: www.ivp.org.au.

Scottish Hillforts Research Program

AOC Archaeology
Edgefield Industrial Estate, Loanhead, Midlothian
Scotland EH20 9SY UK
Tel: ++44 (0131) 440 3593
E-mail: murray.cook@aocarchaeology.com

Desc.:	The project involves a programme of survey and excavation on hillforts across Scotland. These iconic monuments, associated "warring Celts and Picts", are poorly dated and this project specifically aims to excavate and recover dating from as large a sample of these sites as possible over the next few years.
Per.:	1000 BC to 1000 AD.
Country:	Scotland.
Loc.:	Mainland East Coast.
Travel:	Pick-up from Edinburgh and driven to site.
Dur.:	2-8 weeks; June to July.
Age:	Minimum 18.
Qualif.:	No experience necessary.
Work:	Excavation, survey, laboratory work.
Lang.:	English.
Accom.:	Self catering in cottage and flats, about 5 to 10km from the site.
Cost:	GB£195/week. Room & board, travel to and from site and project-related costs included. Transportation to and from Edinburgh and personal expenses not included.
Applic.:	By e-mail, together with CV.
Notes:	The project combines easy relaxed fieldwork training with tours and discussions of specific sites in the evenings.

SECAR — St. Eustatius Center for Archaeological Research

Rosemary Lane, Oranjestad, St Eustatius EUX
Netherlands Antilles, Dutch West Indies
Tel.: ++(599) 524 6770 - Fax: ++(599) 318 3631
E-mail: info@secar.org
www.secar.org

Desc.:	The St. Eustatius Center for Archaeological Research (S.E.C.A.R.) was formed as a not-for-profit research group under the St. Eustatius Historical Foundation on St. Eustatius, Netherlands Antilles in 2000. The S.E.C.A.R. was established to provide a permanent archaeological presence on St. Eustatius with the goal of protecting and developing the historical resources located on the island in full cooperation with local residents.
Per.:	2,500 BC to present.
Country:	Netherlands Anthilles.
Loc.:	St. Eustatius island.
Travel:	Details provided upon application.
Dur.:	Minimum 1 week; January to September.
Age:	Minimum 18.
Qualif.:	No experience necessary.
Work:	Archaeological survey, excavation, collection of findings, drawing, etc.
Lang.:	English.
Accom.:	Various opportunities, from dormitory-style lodging to B&B or hotel. Contact program for further information.
Cost:	US$490/1 week, US$1,435/1 month, US$2,165/2 months.
Applic.:	Online form.

Sedgeford Archaeological and Historical Research Project

Dove House, 32 School Road
Heacham, Norfolk PE31 7DQ UK
Tel.: ++44 (1485) 570 414
E-mail: bookings@sharp.org.uk
www.sharp.org.uk

Desc.: This is among the largest and best-appointed projects for volunteer excavators in the country, setting out to investigate the history and origins of a Norfolk village. The project takes a democratic approach and tries to ensure that everyone understands what is going on and can take part in the process of investigation.

Per.: Middle Saxon to early Medieval.

Country: United Kingdom.

Loc.: Sedgeford, Norfolk.

Travel: Flight to Heathrow (LHR) or Gatwick (LGW) International airport; train to London King's Cross or Liverpool Street; bus or taxi to Sedgeford. Extensive details on how to arrive by car, bike, or foot on website. Further details provided upon application.

Dur.: 1 week; July to August.

Age: Minimum 18; families may be possible.

Qualif.: No experience necessary.

Work: Excavation, training, research.

Lang.: English.

Accom.: Camping with toilets, hot water showers and laundry facilities. B&B's available. Catered meals.

Cost: From GB£20 for day course to GB£100 for week-long course.

Applic.: Online form.

Notes: Several subjects of investigation available with this project.

Semirechie and South Kazakhstan Archaeological Camp

Institute of Geology of Kazakhstan, Laboratory of Geoarchaeology
Tole Bi 21, Room 31, 050010 Almaty Kazakhstan
Tel.: ++7 (7272) 914 386 - Fax: ++7 (7272) 916 111
E-mail: ispkz@nursat.kz
www.cincpac.com/afos/posts/986.html

Desc.:	The Laboratory of Geoarchaeology in cooperation with the State Research Institute on the Cultural Heritage of the Nomads is organising archaeological investigations covering all periods from Palaeolithic to Modern times in Semirechie (Talaz and Almaty).
Per.:	Multi-period; Bronze, Iron and Middle Ages.
Country:	Kazakhstan.
Loc.:	The Chu-Ili Mountains is a semi-desert landscape south-west of Balkhash Lake. The complex of kurgans of Besshatyr is in the Altyn-emel park, 120km (74mi) east of Almaty. The Talas valley is a region among the oldest and richest in monuments in central Asia.
Travel:	Details provided upon application.
Dur.:	15 days to 1 month; July to October.
Age:	Minimum 18.
Qualif.:	Volunteers and archaeology students are welcome.
Work:	Survey, excavation and lectures in the history and archaeology of Central Asia and visits of local sites.
Lang.:	English.
Accom.:	Tents in the field. Alternative options are hotel in Almaty or country houses in the Talas Valley.
Cost:	US$300/week. Transport, food, tent lodging and lectures included. US$30 administration fee for foreigners. Academic credit given by the Institute of Geology and Sri-Nomads.
Applic.:	Contact the project for details. Renewed information available on the Laboratory of Geoarchaeology web site: www.lgakz.org.
Notes:	Anti-tetanus recommended. Valid passport and visa required.

Silchester Roman Town Life Project

Reading University, Department of Archaeology
Whiteknights, PO Box 227, Reading RG6 6AB UK
Tel.: ++44 (118) 378 6255
Fax: ++44 (118) 378 6718
E-mail: a.s.clarke@reading.ac.uk
www.silchester.rdg.ac.uk

Desc.:   A major long-term excavation of a Roman town, run as a training dig for Reading University. Excavations are looking at approximately a third of a single insula, in the heart of the commercial and industrial quarter of the town.

Per.:   Late Iron Age to sub-Roman.

Country: United Kingdom.

Loc.:   Halfway between Reading and Basingstoke.

Travel: See website for specific details.

Dur.:   Minimum 1 week; July to August.

Age.:   Minimum 16.

Qualif.:   The field school is suitable for both beginners and those with some experience.

Work: Urban excavation; volunteering and training.

Lang.:   English.

Accom.:   Camping with running water and hot showers. Volunteer must bring own tent.

Cost: GB£250/6-day week. Food and campsite facilities included. Tent and personal items not included.

Applic.:   Apply to the Department of Archaeology, Reading University.

Notes: Contact Amanda Clarke.

Sino American School

c/o Dr. Alfonz Lengyel
4206 - 73rd Terrace East
Sarasota, Florida 34243 USA
Tel./Fax: ++1 (941) 351 8208
E-mail: fmfsafsa@Juno.com
www.geocities.com/fmfsafsa

Desc.: In 1990, the Fudan Museum Foundation in collaboration with Xi'an Jiaotong University and the Archaeological Research Institute of Shaanxi Province, established the Sino-American Field School of Archaeology (SAFSA). The Education Commission of Shaanxi Province, China and the Society of Professional Archaeologists, USA, accredited the school. Since about 1906, China was closed to foreign archaeologists; SAFSA was the first foreign group that had a permit to excavate in Xi'an together with Chinese archaeologists. Participants have the opportunity to establish future scholarly collaboration with Chinese specialists. The basic principle of the school is not only the summer archaeological practice, but also a good will gesture toward the Chinese people.

Per.: Prehistory (Yangshao) through Tang; about.4,800 BC to AD 907.

Country: China.

Loc.: Shaanxi Province; mainly salvage excavations near Xi'an.

Travel: Flight to Shanghai-Pudong airport (PVG).

Dur.: 1 month; July to August.

Age: Minimum 17.

Qualif.: Open to students (high school seniors, college/university), teachers, professors and a limited number of interested adults.

Work: Excavation practicum, restoration and the study of Chinese cultural history with guest lectures from Chinese specialists.

Lang.: English.

Accom.: Hotels.

Cost: US$3,795 participation fee. Travel expenses between Shanghai

	to Xi'an, tuition and textbook, room & board (3 meals daily, double occupancy lodging), excursions and tour (Shanghai and nearby areas, weekend study tours around Xi'an) included.
Applic.:	Request application form from Dr. Alfonz Lengyel, American Director (fmfsafsa@Juno.com) and return it to the given address with a copy of the photo page of the passport and US$200 down payment for registration fee. First half of the participation fee due April 1st, second half due May 15th by cashier's check payable to Fudan Museum Foundation — SAFSA. Participation is limited to 15.
Notes:	Academic credit given through Xi'an Jiaotong University with approval from home institution. Participants are responsible for their own medical, accident and travel insurance. Consult with appropriate health authorities about vaccination requirements in the home country for travel in China.

Slavia Project

Rybitwy 12, Lednogora, 62-261 Poland
Tel.: ++48 (61) 427 4968
Fax: ++48 (61) 427 5020
E-mail: fieldwork@slavia.org
www.slavia.org

Desc.: Excavations continue at the early Medieval stronghold town of Giecz, whose interior structures include a well-preserved 11th-century stone church, with the only known passage crypt in Poland. Human bone deposits are found in 2 ossuary layers. Students excavate an exterior cemetery site used from 11th to 12th centuries. Grave offerings include knives, decorative heads, rings, coins, amber and bone artefacts. Skeletal preservation is excellent. Beneath the cemetery lie the remains of an earlier tribal settlement, dating to the 8th to 10th centuries.

Per.: Early Medieval; 9th to 11th centuries AD.

Country: Poland.

Loc.: The contemporary village of Giecz, Wielkopolska.

Travel: Details provided upon application.

Dur.: Minimum 2 weeks; June to August.

Age: Minimum 18.

Qualif.: No experience necessary.

Work: Excavation, drawing, record keeping, artefact analysis and handling, mapping and surveying, lectures, tours.

Lang.: English, Polish.

Accom.: Within the Giecz stronghold. Local cuisine; vegetarians welcome.

Cost: Inquire for details. Room & board, local transportation, instruction, field trips, admission fees and equipment included. Airfare not included.

Applic.: Rolling deadline; generally set to March 15th.

Notes: Academic credit available with Adam Mickiewicz Univ., Poznan.

Sortino — Necropolis of Pantalica

Legambiente
Via Salaria 403, 00199 Rome Italy
Tel.: ++39 (06) 8626 8323
Fax: ++39 (06) 2332 5776
E-mail: volontariato@legambiente.eu
www.legambiente.eu/volontariato/campi

Desc.:	The camp will take place in Pantalica, listed as Unesco world heritage site owing to the 5000 old graves located on the chalky rock faces that give this place a unique aspect.
Per.:	9th to 8th centuries BC.
Country:	Italy.
Loc.:	Sortino, Siracusa.
Travel:	By bus from Siracusa or from Catania.
Dur.:	12 days; July to August.
Age:	Minimum 18.
Qualif.:	No experience necessary.
Work:	The work is strictly related to the implementation and use of the necropolis: volunteers will work on clearing bushes and weeds from a path and raising awareness activities among tourists. The coast and surrounding areas can be visited during free time.
Lang.:	Italian.
Accom.:	Dormitory style accommodation.
Cost:	EUR215 plus membership fee.
Applic.:	Inquire for instructions. See also: Legambiente.

The Speaker's House

151 W. Main Street
PO Box 26686
College, PA 19426 USA
Tel.: ++1 (610) 489 2105
E-mail: info@speakershouse.org
www.speakershouse.org

Desc.:	The purpose of the archaeological research is to inform the interpretation of the site, which is most noteworthy for being the home of Frederick Muhlenberg (1750-1801), first Speaker of the House of Representatives.
Per.:	1700-2000.
Country:	United States.
Loc.:	Collegeville, Pennsylvania.
Travel:	Flight to Philadelphia International Airport (PHL). Public transportation to Collegeville.
Dur.:	2-6 weeks; June to July.
Age:	Minimum 18.
Qualif.:	No experience necessary.
Work:	Excavation, survey and laboratory work.
Lang.:	English.
Accom.:	College dorms, just over 1mi (2km) from the site.
Cost:	US$520/2-week session; US$520 for each subsequent session. Room & board not included. Transportation, airport departure tax and personal expenses not included. Costs are subject to change.
Applic.:	E-mail or telephone to request application.

Stara Zagora Heritage Workcamp

Balkan Heritage (BH) Field School
204 Sveta Troica str.
BG-6004 Stara Zagora Bulgaria
Tel.: ++359 (42) 235 402 /888 165 402
E-mail: balkanheritage@gmail.com
www.bhfieldschool.org

Desc.:	Stara Zagora Regional History Museum has implemented an intensive excavation workcamp programme focused on rescue sectors, where mainly Roman and Late Antique layers are to be studied, and local archaeological sites that are already opened to visitors. Volunteers will support the Museum with the rescue excavations and the maintenance of archaeological sites. They will also be involved in the development of advocacy campaign "Keep the heritage alive", aiming to raise public awareness towards cultural heritage protection and volunteer involvement.
Per.:	Roman to Late Antique; 107-590 AD.
Country:	Bulgaria.
Loc.:	Stara Zagora (south-central region).
Travel:	Transfer from the nearest airports of Sofia and Burgas is available. Otherwise, participants may travel by train or bus.
Dur.:	2 weeks; July and August.
Age:	Minimum 16.
Qualif.:	No experience necessary.
Work:	Excavation, survey, maintenance of archaeological sites, campaigning.
Lang.:	English.
Accom.:	Hotel rooms with WC, showers, air-conditioning, TV.
Cost:	EUR399/2 weeks (-15% for each subsequent project), room & board, excursions, sightseeing tours, entrance fees, workshops, medical insurance and administrative costs.
Applic.:	Online form.

Tel Dor Archaeological Project

Institute of Archaeology, Hebrew University of Jerusalem
Mt. Scopus 91950, Jerusalem Israel
Tel.: ++972 (2) 588 1304
Fax: ++972 (2) 582 5548
E-mail: dor-proj@mscc.huji.ac.il
www.dor.huji.ac.il

Desc.: The Tel Dor project is devoted to investigating one of the largest coastal cities in ancient Israel. Tel Dor (Kh. el-Burj), is identified with D[y]r of Egyptian sources, Biblical Dor and with Dor/Dora of Greek and Roman sources. The port dominated the fortunes of the town throughout its 3000-odd year history. Excavations were carried out in the 1920s and then from 1980 onwards. The current consortium uses the site as a testing ground for new techniques and technologies for extracting information about the past.

Per.: Bronze and Iron Ages, Persian, Hellenistic and Roman periods.

Country: Israel.

Loc.: Israel's Mediterranean coast, about 19mi (30km) south of Haifa.

Travel: Train from the Ben-Gurion Airport northward to Bat Galim station.

Dur.: 2-5 weeks; July and August.

Age: Minimum 16.

Qualif.: No previous experience necessary.

Work: Participants will be engaged in all facets of state-of-the-art field archaeology, including excavation, digital registration of architecture and artefacts, analysis of finds and stratigraphy and site conservation and will gain proficiency in these subjects as they work closely with the professional and academic staff.

Lang.: English, Hebrew.

Accom.: At Kfar Galim, a boarding school near Haifa (15min. drive from Dor).

Cost: EUR2,100/full season; EUR1,300/half-season. Discounts available.

Applic.: Online. Deadline for registration May 15th.

Tel Hazor Excavations Project

Institute of Archaeology, The Hebrew University of Jerusalem
Mount Scopus Jerusalem 91905 Israel
Tel.: ++972 (2) 588 2403 /4
Fax: ++972 (2) 582 5548
E-mail: hazor@huji.ac.il
http://hazor.huji.ac.il

Desc.:	Hazor is an ancient Canaanite and Israelite city located in the north of modern day Israel. It is the largest biblical-era site in Israel, covering some 200 acres. Once an important city in the region, Hazor is comprised of the upper city (the acropolis) and the lower city (the fortified enclosure) lying close to the north.
Per.:	Early to Late Bronze Age; 3rd millennium BC, 18th to 13th centuries BC. Iron Age: 12th to 8th centuries BC.
Country:	Israel.
Loc.:	Hazor is about 3mi (5km) north of Rosh-Pinnah, northern Israel.
Travel:	Bus from Ben-Gurion Airport, Jerusalem, Tel Aviv or Haifa to Rosh Pinnah Junction. Transport provided to the camp.
Dur.:	6 weeks; June 21st to July 31st.
Age:	Minimum 18.
Qualif.:	No experience necessary.
Work:	Excavations at the site; 5:00 to 14:00, Monday through Friday, with additional work assignments in the afternoon and the evenings. Lectures during the week provide training in field archaeology and interpretation of finds.
Lang.:	English, Hebrew.
Accom.:	Kibbutz Kefar-Hanassi Village Inn: 3 persons/room, equipped with air conditioning, refrigerator, microwave, cable TV. Kibbutz offers swimming-pool, basketball and tennis courts, large supermarket.
Cost:	US$1,200/session (US$400/week) or US$2,200 for full 6-week term, payable at Hazor. Bring a modest amount of money to cover personal expenses and additional travel before and after

the dig.

Applic: Print online form and mail to Prof. Amnon Ben-Tor including US$75 registration fee (include a return address). All payments if made by check (personal, travellers' checks, bankers' checks) should be made in the applicant's national currency. (Note: remittance must be by check or money order payable to: The Israel Exploration Society, PO Box 7041, Jerusalem 91070 Israel; tel. ++972 (2) 625 7991; fax: ++972 (2) 624 7772; e-mail: ies@vms.huji.ac.il; www.hum.huji.ac.il/ies/).

Notes: Academic credit available through the Rothberg School at the Hebrew University of Jerusalem. See also: Hebrew University of Jerusalem.

Tell es-Safi/Gath Archaeological Project

The Institute of Archaeology, Martin (Szusz) Department of Land of
Israel Studies and Archaeology
Bar Ilan University, Ramat-Gan, 52900 Israel
Fax: ++972 (3) 535 1233
E-mail: maeira@mail.biu.ac.il
www.dig-gath.org; http://gath.wordpress.com

Desc.:	Tell es-Safi, the Biblical City of "Gath of the Philistines" (home of biblical Goliath and Achish), is among the largest tells (ancient ruin mounds) and most important sites in Israel. Finds include inscriptions, siege system, destruction level and cultural facets.
Per.:	Proto-historic through Modern with focus on Bronze and Iron Ages; 3rd to 1st millennium BC.
Country:	Israel.
Loc.:	At border between Philistia and Judean foothills (Shephelah) in central Israel, on southern bank of Elah Valley in the Southern Levant, about halfway between Jerusalem and Ashkelon.
Travel:	Details provided upon application.
Dur.:	2-4 weeks; July to August.
Age:	Minimum 16.
Qualif.:	No experience necessary.
Work:	Excavation, post-excavation (e.g., pottery washing), lectures, field trips. Sunday afternoon to Friday afternoon.
Lang.:	English.
Accom.:	Kibbutz Revadim with air-conditioned rooms, pool, kosher food.
Cost:	US$50 application fee plus US$375/week or US$1,500/4 weeks; room & board and project transport included. Travel, insurance and laundry not included. Academic credit with additional fees.
Applic.:	Deadline May 1st. Registration finalized upon receipt of insurance, "conduct and behaviour" forms and US$750 by bank check made out to "Israel Exploration Society" (US funds only, no money transfers). Balance due 1st day of participation.

UNAREC — Union Nationale des Associations Régionales Etudes & Chantiers

33, rue Campagne Première
75014 Paris France
Tel.: ++33 (1) 4538 9626
E-mail: unarec@wanadoo.fr
www.unarec.org

Desc.:	UNAREC organises international workcamps for adults and teenagers as well as a programme working with people facing social or economical difficulties. In 1997 it became involved with EVS and since 1962 has been working with many partners around the world. Volunteers participate in projects such as restoring a village bread oven, cleaning riverbanks, organising festivals and cultural activities.
Per.:	Various.
Country:	Africa, Asia, Europe, Middle East, Latin and North America.
Travel:	Details provided upon application to specific project.
Dur.:	Varies with project; year round.
Age:	Minimum 18; 14-17 for youth workcamps.
Qualif.:	No specific qualifications needed .
Work:	Community development, construction, culture, environment. Several archaeological projects listed on website.
Lang.:	French; English is often used on adult workcamps since there may be many nationalities.
Accom.:	Varies with project.
Cost:	EUR135-150 registration fee; EUR250-360 placement fee. Room & board and insurance included. Travel costs not included.
Applic.:	Non-French volunteers contact the partner organisation in home country (see website). Volunteers from a country without a partner organisation contact the UNAREC international office: D.I. UNAREC, 3 rue des Petits Gras - F-63000 Clermont-Ferrand; tel.: ++33 (4) 7331 9804; fax: ++33 (4) 7331 9809; email: unarec.di@wanadoo.fr.

Underwater Archaeology in the Mediterranean Sea

Ecomuseum of the Cape of Cavalleria and the Sa Nitja Association
PO Box: APDO 68, 07740 Es Mercadal, Menorca Spain
Tel./Fax: ++34 (971) 359 999 - Mob.: ++34 (608) 894 650
E-mail: sanisera@arrakis.es
www.ecomuseodecavalleria.com

Desc.:	This study explores the Roman port of Sanitja and the coast of the Cape of Cavalleria identifying structures from the Roman city of Sanisera as well as shipwrecks. Ruins of a Muslim mosque and English defence tower offer potential to find vessels from these periods. Excursions will teach the history and culture of Menorca.
Per.:	Early Roman to Modern.
Country:	Spain.
Loc.:	Cape of Cavalleria, Es Mercadal, Menorca, The Balearic Islands.
Travel:	Details provided upon application.
Dur.:	14 days/session; 4 sessions; May and October-November.
Age:	Minimum 18.
Qualif.:	Group 1: No open-water diving certificate. Group 2: Open-water diving certificate from an internationally recognized organisation.
Work:	Experience in underwater archaeological field work (site discovery, lab analysis), surveying methods, site reconnaissance, recording, drawing, mapping, position fixing, photograph, lab processing. Lectures on Roman archaeology. 6hrs/day, 6 days/week.
Lang.:	English and Spanish.
Accom.:	Student residence (air-conditioned) in town of Ciutadella within walking distance of the historic centre, port and beaches.
Cost:	US$1,950-2,300 (subject to change); room & board, transportation, insurance, planned excursions, application fee and administrative costs included. Travel expenses not included.
Applic.:	E-mail or online form with US$250 deposit. Balance due 30 days in advance. See also: Necropolis of the Roman City of Sanisera.

Underwater Archaeology International Field School

IAS - Istituto Attività Subacquee
Via E. Amari 7, 90144 Palermo Italy
Tel.: ++39 (091) 730 3046 - Mob.: ++39 (335) 451 533
E-mail: Marcello@infcom.it
www.istitutoattivitasubacque.it

Desc.: IAS (Institute for underwater activities) is a cultural association that organises courses and fieldschools in underwater archaeology, in Italy as well as in Libya, Romania (Black Sea) and Serbia.

Per.: Classic, Roman, Medieval (Arab period).

Country: Italy.

Loc.: San Vito Lo Capo; western Sicily; Cyrenaic Libya.

Travel: Plane, train or boat to Palermo, then bus to San Vito Lo Capo.

Dur.: 3 weeks; May to October.

Age.: Minimum 18.

Qualif.: No previous experience required.

Work: Daily activities (on sites indicated by local authorities): prospecting, air-lift excavation, soundings, graphic surveys, photography, drawing, mapping. Lesson topics: introduction to archaeology and underwater archaeology, ancient trade and naval construction, methods of archaeological research, analysis of archives and bibliographic sources, archaeological drawing and surveying.

Lang.: English, Italian.

Accom.: Tourist apartments for 2-4 people.

Cost: EUR680/1 week; EUR980/2 weeks; EUR1,300/3 weeks. Room & board included.

Applic.: Via e-mail plus a deposit of 30% of participation fee.

Notes: Divers are supervised by a specialist in hyperbaric medicine, who checks their health condition daily. IAS also offers training for a licence for "Archaeology Instructor" recognised by NASE (National Academy of Scuba Educator) - see website.

UNESCO — United Nations Educational, Scientific and Cultural Organization

7, place de Fontenoy
75352 Paris 07 SP France
Tel.: ++33 (1) 4568 1000
Fax: ++33 (1) 4567 1690
www.unesco.org

Desc.:   UNESCO was established in 1945. It has its headquarters in Paris, France, and many field offices and units in different parts of the world. The goal of this international body is to mobilise governments and other international partners in favour of voluntary service to make more programmes, projects, funding and other support for young people available. In this way young people around the world will be encouraged and aided in becoming volunteers and being responsible actors in their societies.

Per.:   Various.

Country: Worldwide.

Loc.:   Various.

Travel: Details provided upon application to project organisation.

Dur.:   Typically minimum 2 weeks.

Age: 18-25.

Qualif.:   No experience necessary.

Work: Diverse programmes available in a wide range of sectors including archaeology and culture.

Lang.:   English or language of host country.

Accom.:   Variable.

Cost: Inquire with project organisation.

Applic.:   UNESCO does not recruit volunteers or organise volunteer programmes, workcamps or exchanges.

Union REMPART

1, rue des Guillemites, 75004 Paris France
Tel.: ++33 (1) 4271 9655
Fax: ++33 (1) 4271 7300
E-mail: contact@rempart.com
International officer: duffaud@rempart.com;
www.rempart.com

Desc.:	REMPART, a union of heritage renovation projects associations, organises short voluntary work schemes mainly in France. The projects are all based around restoration and maintenance of historic sites and buildings, from a glamorous French chateau to a picturesque ruined village. Renovation projects around the world are also available on specific conditions.
Per.:	Various.
Country:	Worldwide.
Loc.:	Various.
Travel:	Details provided upon application.
Dur.:	2 weeks; year round.
Age:	Minimum 17 or 18.
Qualif.:	Previous voluntary experience is not necessarily required.
Work:	Restoration; usually 30-35 hrs/week.
Lang.:	French.
Accom.:	Basic accommodations; varies with each camp.
Cost:	About GB£8 (approximately US$13)/day; room & board included. Costs and currency exchange rates subject to change.
Applic.:	Contact the organisation.

USCAP — University of Sydney Central Asian Programme

Archaeology in Central Asia
Archaeology A14, University of Sydney NSW 2006 Australia
Tel.: ++61 (2) 9351 2090 - Fax:++61 (2) 9351 7760
E-mail: alison.betts@archaeology.usyd.edu.au
www.acl.arts.usyd.edu.ay/central_asia

Desc.:	USCAP in collaboration with the Institute of History, Archaeology and Ethnography (IHAE), Karakalpak Academy of Sciences takes a field team on archaeological excavations in Uzbekistan and a trip through the Medieval Silk Road cities.
Per.:	4th century BC to 2nd century AD.
Country:	Uzbekistan.
Loc.:	Excavation headquarters in ancient Chorasmia, the western province of modern Uzbekistan, set facing a dune-field covering the ruined city of Kazakl'i-yatkan.
Travel:	All arrangements made by tour organisers.
Dur.:	Approximately 3 weeks; September.
Age:	Minimum 18.
Qualif.:	No experience necessary.
Work:	Excavation, drawing, planning, cleaning features, recording finds.
Lang.:	English.
Accom.:	Excavation headquarters (13 nights) in dormitory style accommodation, with electricity, hot showers and outdoor "squat" toilets. Cooking and cleaning provided. Modern guest houses and 3-star hotels during tours.
Cost:	Approx. AUS$6,200 Sydney/Brisbane/Melbourne; GB£1,400 or US$2,200 land only (exchange rates subject to change). Prices vary to consider international flights, departure taxes, meals in Uzbekistan, guided tours and sight-seeing.
Applic.:	For bookings and cost information, contact Odyssey Travel at www.odysseytravel.com.au, otherwise contact USCAP.

Valley of Peace Archaeological Project

University of Illinois at Urbana-Champaign
109 Davenport Hall, Urbana, IL 61801 USA
Tel.: ++1 (217) 333 3616
Fax: ++1 (217) 244 3490
E-mail: ljlucero@uiuc.edu

Desc.:	The on-going research of this project is exploring how early Maya rulers replicated and expanded household rituals to acquire political power. The excavations focus on collecting ritual data, particularly information on termination, dedication, renewal and ancestor veneration rituals.
Per.:	Classic Maya; 250-850 AD.
Country:	Belize.
Loc.:	Yalbac, central Belize.
Travel:	Detail provided upon application.
Dur.:	5 weeks; May to June.
Age:	Minimum 18.
Qualif.:	No experience necessary.
Work:	Survey and excavation, 5 days per week.
Lang.:	English.
Accom.:	Inquire for details.
Cost:	Approximately US$4,500. Tuition, transportation to and from Belize and room & board included.
Applic.:	Via e-mail only. Contact the project director Dr. Lisa Lucero.
Notes:	Academic credit available with approval from home university. A list will be provided of necessary equipment, clothing, paperwork and vaccinations.

Villasmundo — Melilli

Legambiente
Via Salaria 403, 00199 Rome Italy
Tel.: ++39 (06) 8626 8323
Fax: ++39 (06) 2332 5776
E-mail: volontariato@legambiente.eu
www.legambiente.eu/volontariato/campi

Desc.:	The Peraro archaeological site, in which there are ruins from the Bronze Age, shows evidences of the ancient Greek colonisation and is characterised by a beautiful landscape and an amazing view over the cities and mountains nearby.
Per.:	9th to 8th centuries BC.
Country:	Italy.
Loc.:	Melilli, Siracusa.
Travel:	Bus from Siracusa or from Catania.
Dur.:	15 days; July.
Age:	Minimum 18.
Qualif.:	No experience necessary.
Work:	After training, volunteers will collaborate with the local staff in cleaning the site and carrying out archaeological research in the area.
Lang.:	English.
Accom.:	In school.
Cost:	EUR190 plus membership fee.
Applic.:	Inquire for instructions. See also: Legambiente

Vindolanda Trust

Chesterholm Museum
Bardon Mill, Hexham
Northumberland NE47 7JN UK
Tel.: ++44 (1434) 344 277 - Fax: ++44 (1434) 344 060
E-mail: info@vindolanda.com
www.vindolanda.com

Desc.: The Vindolanda "vicus," or Roman town outside the last fort at Vindolanda 212-300 century AD, is among the best explored in Roman Britain and Empire as a whole, yet at least half of the area is believed to contain the 3rd-century town and late cemeteries yet to be explored. Trenches will be cut to explore the earlier military remains from the pre-Hadrianic era, including the exploration of a deep fort ditch and locate features from the 2nd century.

Per.: Roman; 100-300 AD.

Country: United Kingdom.

Loc.: Hexham Northumberland. About the centre of Hadrian's Wall near the village of Bardon Mill, 2mi (3km) behind the Wall.

Travel: Volunteers must provide own travel. There are some public transport but irregular. From the international airport in Newcastle-Upon-Tyne, take subway or taxi to the Once Brewed Youth Hostel or the Hayden Bridge Lodge in Vindolanda.

Dur.: 5-day sessions; April to September.

Age: Minimum 16.

Qualif.: No experience necessary.

Work: Excavation of Roman fort and vicus.

Lang.: English.

Accom.: Information about local accommodation available on website. The Youth Hostel is within walking distance from the project.

Cost: GB£50/2 weeks plus GB£15 membership to the "Friends of Vindolanda".

Applic.: E-mail or regular mail online form. See website for details.

Vive Mexico

Morelia, Michoacan, Boulevard Garcia de Leon 734-A
Fraccionamiento Chapultepec Oriente
CP 58280 Mexico
Tel./Fax: ++521 (443) 324 5170
E-mail: international@vivemexico.org
www.vivemexico.org

Desc.: Founded in 1994 and legally constituted in 1997, Vive Mexico was born as an initiative of students from the Economics Faculty at the Michoacan University. It is the first organisation legally constituted in Mexico and had became the biggest organisation in Latin America dedicated to promoting international co-operation and the development of the International Voluntary Service Activities, coordinating short-, medium- and long-term projects as well as special co-operations between Mexico and more than 45 countries worldwide. It had also coordinated a wide variety of seminars and conferences as well as leadership training.

Per.: Modern/contemporary.

Country: Mexico.

Loc.: Various locations in Mexico and Latin America.

Travel: From Mexico City international airport (MEX) detailed travel instructions will be provided.

Dur.: 3 weeks to 1 year.

Age: Minimum 18.

Qualif.: No experience necessary.

Work: Cultural, social and ecological projects.

Lang.: English, Spanish is recommended.

Accom.: Houses, youth centres or tents; varies with project.

Cost: EUR190-210/3 weeks, room & board, international guide, local coordination of activities and administrative expenses included.

Applic.: E-mail for more information about activities and projects.

Volunteer Latin America

PO Box 585
Rochester ME1 9EJ UK
Tel.: ++44 (20) 7193 9163
E-mail: info@volunteerlatinamerica.com
www.volunteerlatinamerica.com

Desc.: Volunteer Latin America is a comprehensive source of free and low-cost volunteering opportunities in Central and South America, offering a customised information service for people of all ages and nationalities on voluntary work opportunities in the environmental and humanitarian sectors. They also provide information on recommended Spanish language schools in Central and South America and offer advice on how to set up a volunteer placement.

Per.: Various; depends on project.

Country: Central and South America.

Loc.: Various.

Travel: Details provided upon application.

Dur.: Each project stipulates a fixed term contract or requires a minimum commitment. This might be a number of weeks or months.

Age: Minimum 18.

Qualif.: Generally, most projects do not require any special qualifications.

Work: Recovering and identifying of petroglyphs and related archaeological sites, mapping archaeological sites, drawing and photographing petroglyphs, etc. Volunteers with no archaeological experience are trained in petroglyph recording techniques.

Lang.: English.

Accom.: Depends on project.

Cost: Depends on project. Some require a small financial contribution whereas others provide free room & board.

Applic.: Details should be acquired from the chosen organisation.

Volunteers for Peace International Voluntary Service

1034 Tiffany Road, Belmont Vermont 05730 USA
Tel.: ++1 (802) 259 2759
Fax: ++1 (802) 259 2922
E-mail: vfp@vfp.org
www.vfp.org

Desc.:	This non-profit membership organisation has been coordinating international workcamps since 1982. It is a member of CCIVS at UNESCO and works in cooperation with SCI, Alliance of European Voluntary Service Organisations and YAP (see listings).
Per.:	Various.
Country:	Various; Africa, Asia, Europe, the Americas, Middle East, Oceania.
Loc.:	Varies with project.
Travel:	Varies with project and is arranged and paid for by the volunteer.
Dur.:	2-3 weeks; year round, but typically June to September.
Age:	Minimum 18. Teen camps for volunteers under 18.
Qualif.:	No experience necessary.
Work:	Varies with project; excavation, field survey, restoration, etc.
Lang.:	English.
Accom.:	Project accommodations vary greatly.
Cost:	Registration fee of US$300 per project (US$500 for volunteers under 18) plus mandatory membership of US$30. Room & board included. Russian, African, Asian and Latin American programmes may cost an additional fee of US$300-500.
Applic.:	Download VFP registration form from the VFP website and e-mail, fax or mail form to VFP along with VFP registration fee. A penalty of US$150 is charged for changing projects after registering.
Notes:	Placement of nationals of countries other than the United States and Canada may be possible only if a partner organisation in the home country of the applicant does not exist.

Wadi ath-Thamad Project

Wilfrid Laurier University
Waterloo, Ontario N2L 3C5 Canada
Tel.: ++1 (519) 884 1970 Ext. 6680
Fax: ++1 (519) 884 8853
E-mail: mdaviau@wlu.ca
www.wlu.ca/~wwwarch/jordan/

Desc.:   This project involves several, a Roman castellum and most importantly at the site of Khirbat al-Mudayna. This Iron Age site is a fortified town with features including a casemate wall, a 6-chambered gate building with standing stones at the entrance, a temple and a 3-pillared building used for industrial purposes. Other buildings of interest in the area date to the early Roman period, with evidence of Nabataean culture.

Per.:   Iron Age, Nabataean, early Roman.

Country: Jordan.

Loc.:   11mi (18km) from the town of Madaba.

Travel: Details provided upon application.

Dur.:   6 weeks; June to August.

Age: Minimum 18.

Qualif.:   No experience necessary.

Work: Excavation and survey.

Lang.:   English.

Accom.:   The Black Iris Hotel and Lulu's Pension.

Cost: CAD$2,500 plus CAD$50 application fee for Canadians; US$2,200 plus US$50 for non-Canadian team members per season. Lodging and 4 meals/day included. Airfare not included.

Applic.:   Deadline March 5th. Contact Dr. P. M. Michele Daviau for further instructions.

Notes: The project does not take place every year. Please check the website for further details. Prices may vary from year to year.

Waterway Recovery Group

Island House, Moor Road
Chesham, HP5 1WA UK
Tel.: ++44 (1494) 783 453
E-mail: enquiries@wrg.org.uk
www.wrg.org.uk

Desc.: Volunteers are needed to restore Britain's derelict canals with the national co-ordinating body for voluntary labour on the inland waterways of Great Britain.

Per.: 18th to 19th centuries.

Country: United Kingdom.

Loc.: Various.

Travel: Details of the camp along with travel directions are sent a few weeks in advance. Pick-up at a nearby coach or train station is arranged.

Dur.: Minimum 1 day, weekend or weeklong opportunities; year round.

Age: Minimum 18; maximum 70. Volunteer must be over 21 if English is a second language.

Qualif.: No experience necessary.

Work: Work may involve restoring industrial archaeology, demolishing old brickwork, driving a dump truck, clearing mud and vegetation and helping at a National Waterways festival. Work may be either on weekends or weeklong canal camps.

Lang.: English.

Accom.: A village hall, sports centre or similar style accommodation. Bring sleeping bag and mat.

Cost: GB£49/week or GB£7/day. Includes room & board.

Applic.: Contact the Enquiries Officer at the above address.

Notes: Physically and mentally disabled volunteers may apply.

Whitehall Farm

University of Northampton
Simon's Cottage, Stowe Hill, Weedon
Northants NN7 4SF UK
Tel.: ++44 (1604) 637 763 - Mob.: ++44 (0783) 584 2840
E-mail: info@whitehallvilla.com
www.whitehallvilla.co.uk

Desc.:	Volunteers are involved in the excavation of a Romano-British villa concentrating on structural elements of an estate bath-house. The "dig" is a community-based initiative and is part of a 10-year research programme into a multi-period site. The excavation forms an important focal point for characterising the wider area of Roman settlements.
Per.:	Roman.
Country:	United Kingdom.
Loc.:	Near Junction 16 of M1, Northamptonshire.
Travel:	Details provided upon application.
Dur.:	2-4 weeks; June 15th to July 12th.
Age:	Minimum 18.
Qualif.:	No experience necessary. Training provided.
Work:	Excavation, planning, surveying, finds processing, archiving and training. Volunteers are expected to help with a public Open Day on the 12th July.
Lang.:	English.
Accom.:	B&B's and hotels in village. Pubs and shops in walking distance.
Cost:	None.
Applic.:	Online form by May 1st. Contact Sandra Deacon.

YAP — Youth Action for Peace

International Secretariat
3, Avenue du Parc Royal
1020 Bruxelles Belgium
Tel.: ++32 (2) 478 9410 - Fax: ++32 (2) 478 9432
E-mail: info@yap.org
www.yap.org

Desc.:	YAP facilitates international workcamps in archaeological, environmental and conservation of parks, gardening, culture and development projects.
Per.:	Various.
Country:	Throughout the Mediterranean, America, Asia and Africa.
Loc.:	Various.
Travel:	Details provided upon application to specific project.
Dur.:	1-4 weeks, longer projects may be 3-12 months; year round.
Age:	Minimum 18 (some projects for teenagers).
Qualif.:	No experience necessary.
Work:	Restoration, reconstruction, maintenance, public outreach, etc.
Lang.:	English or language of host country.
Accom.:	Varies from camping to hostelling; typically group settings.
Cost:	Small registration fee and travel costs.
Applic.:	Contact most convenient branch (see website).

Yavneh-Yam Archaeological Project

The Ayanot Agricultural School
D.N. Emeq Soreq 70490 Israel
Tel.: ++972 (8) 940 4655 /940 4635 /940 4682 /940 5558
Fax: ++972 (8) 940 4785
E-mail: ilansh@netvision.net.il
www.tau.ac.il./~yavneyam/

Desc.: Yavneh-Yam has been occupied since early antiquity, as revealed both by historical sources and archaeological evidence. The site is mentioned for the first time as "muhazzi" in 15th century BC Egyptian sources and later on as "the harbour of the people of Iamnia"(Yavneh-Yam). In Middle Age maps it is denominated "the harbour of the Jews".

Per.: Middle to Late Bronze Age, Iron Age, Persian, Hellenistic, Roman, Byzantine and Early Islamic periods; 9th century BC to 7th century AD.

Country: Israel.

Loc.: Yavneh-Yam, the harbour of Jewish inland city Yavneh, equidistant (about 12.5mi/20km) between Jaffa and Ashdod.

Travel: Details provided upon application.

Dur.: Minimum 1 week; July to August.

Age: Minimum 16.

Qualif.: No experience necessary.

Work: Excavation, cleaning, surveying, finds processing, archiving.

Lang.: English.

Accom.: Youth village Ayanot (10-minute drive from the site) with 4 people per room and air conditioning, bathroom and shower. Modern dining hall with a large variety of Israeli/Near Eastern cuisine.

Cost: US$450/week. Airfare not included.

Applic.: Online form.

APPENDICES

ORGANISATIONS AND PROJECTS

ANALYTICAL TABLE BY GEOGRAPHIC AREAS AND PERIODS

Organisation / Project	Europe – Prehistory	Europe – Classic/Iron Age	Europe – Roman	Europe – Early Medieval	Europe – Medieval	Europe – Renaissance/Post Medieval	Europe – Early Modern	Europe – Modern	Europe – Contemporary	Europe – Multiperiod	Middle East – Prehistory	Middle East – Greek-Roman	Middle East – Islamic/Medieval/Cont.	Asia – Prehistory	Asia – Far East Civilisations	Asia – Modern/Contemporary	Africa – Prehistory/Palaeonthology	Africa – Modern/Contemporary	North America – Prehistory/Palaeonthol.	North America – Early Cultures	North America – Modern/Conemporary	Latin America – Prehistory	Latin America – Maya/Precolombian	Latin America – Pre-Inca/Inca	Latin America – Colonial/Modern	Caribbean	Oceania	Worldwide
Aang Serian Peace Village																		X										
Achill Archaeological Field School	X																											
ADMAT – The Tile Wreck Maritime Archaeological Project (1720's)						X	X			X																X		
African Legacy																	X	X										
AIEP – Ass. for Ed.,Cult and Work Int. Exchange Programs													X				X	X										X
Alliance of European Voluntary Service Organisations										X																		
Alutiiq Museum and Achaeological Repository																			X	X								
Amphora Graveyard of Monte Testaccio			X																									
Anatolian Archaeology Field School											X	X	X															
Ancient Metal Production and History in Southern Jordan											X	X	X															
Aramus Excavations and Fieldschool											X	X	X															
Archaeolink Prehistory Park	X	X																										
Archaeological Excavations in Northern Spain		X	X																									
Archaeological Field Methods Field School			X																									
Archaeology at Ben Lomond								X																				
Archaeology Field Research Program																			X	X	X							
ArchaeoSpain – The Roman Theater of Clunia			X				X																					
Archeodig Project - Researching a Roman Coastal Settlement on Poggio del Molino, Populonia			X	X																								
Archeostage – Olloy-Sur-Viroin Archaeological Dig		X																										
ArcheoVenezia Archaeological Field Work Camp					X																							

226

ORGANISATIONS AND PROJECTS

ANALYTICAL TABLE BY GEOGRAPHIC AREAS AND PERIODS

Organisation / Project	Worldwide	Oceania	Caribbean	Latin America – Colonial/Modern	Latin America – Pre-Inca/Inca	Latin America – Maya/Precolombian	Latin America – Prehistory	North America – Modern/Contemporary	North America – Early Cultures	North America – Prehistory/Palaeonthol.	Africa – Modern/Contemporary	Africa – Prehistory/Palaeonthology	Asia – Modern/Contemporary	Asia – Far East Civilisations	Asia – Prehistory	Middle East – Islamic/Medieval/Cont.	Middle East – Greek-Roman	Middle East – Prehistory	Europe – Multiperiod	Europe – Contemporary	Europe – Modern	Europe – Early Modern	Europe – Renaissance/Post Medieval	Europe – Medieval	Europe – Early Medieval	Europe – Roman	Europe – Classic/Iron Age	Europe – Prehistory
ASEPAM																				X							X	
Augusta Trajana-Beroe-Borui Rescue Excavations Project	X																			X						X	X	
AVSO – Association of Voluntary Service Organisations	X																											
Baga Gazaryn Chuluu Excavation														X	X													
Balkan Heritage Field School														X					X		X	X	X		X			
Bamburgh Research Project																			X			X	X		X	X		
Bektashi Tekke of Melan, Albania																			X			X	X					
Belize Valley Archaeology Reconnaissance Project						X																						
Bitola Heritage Workcamp																											X	X
Bra_ov Project								X	X	X																	X	X
Build Your Own PIT Project								X	X	X																		
Bunifat Project																			X						X	X		
Butser Ancient Farm																			X						X	X	X	
Caer Alyn Archaeological and Heritage Project																			X		X	X	X		X	X	X	
Canterbury Archaeological Trust Ltd.																			X			X	X		X	X	X	
Capena Excavation Project																										X	X	
Carnuntum																										X		
Castanheiro Do Vento																												X
Castell Henllys Training Excavation																										X	X	
CCIVS – Coordinating Committee for International Volunteers	X																											
Chateau Ganne																								X				
Cirò Archaeological Field Work Camp																									X			X

ORGANISATIONS AND PROJECTS

ANALYTICAL TABLE BY GEOGRAPHIC AREAS AND PERIODS

Organisation / Project	Europe – Prehistory	Europe – Classic/Iron Age	Europe – Roman	Europe – Early Medieval	Europe – Medieval	Europe – Renaissance/Post Medieval	Europe – Early Modern	Europe – Modern	Europe – Contemporary	Europe – Multiperiod	Middle East – Prehistory	Middle East – Greek-Roman	Middle East – Islamic/Medieval/Cont.	Asia – Prehistory	Asia – Far East Civilisations	Asia – Modern/Contemporary	Africa – Prehistory/Palaeonthology	Africa – Modern/Contemporary	North America – Prehistory/Palaeonthol.	North America – Early Cultures	North America – Modern/Contemporary	Latin America – Prehistory	Latin America – Maya/Precolombian	Latin America – Pre-Inca/Inca	Latin America – Colonial/Modern	Caribbean	Oceania	Worldwide
Club du Vieux Manoir					X	X	X	X		X																		
Compagnons Batisseurs							X			X																		
Concordia			X							X																		X
Copped Hall Trust Archaeological Project	X	X			X	X																						
Cornell Halai and East Lokris Project						X				X																		
Cotravaux										X																		X
Council for British Archaeology										X																		
Crow Canyon Archaeological Center																				X								
CVE – Caribbean Volunteer Expeditions																										X		
Czech American Archaeological Field School in Premyslovice Neolithic Village				X						X																		
Discovering Italy's Ancient Roman Coast			X	X																								
Dispilio Excavations	X																											
Earthwatch Institute																												X
Eco-Archaeological Park Pontecagnano Faiano		X																										
El Pilar Archaeological Reserve for Maya Flora and Fauna																							X					
Elix – Conservation Volunteers Greece										X																		
Excavations at Kalavasos-Kokkinoyia	X																											
Excavations at St. Mary Magdalen Leper Hospital, Winchester							X			X																		
Falerii – Via Amerina		X	X																									
Farnese – Rofalco		X																										
Field School in East-Central Europe							X																					
Fiji's Ancient Seafarers																											X	

228

ORGANISATIONS AND PROJECTS

ANALYTICAL TABLE BY GEOGRAPHIC AREAS AND PERIODS

Organisation / Project	Europe – Prehistory	Europe – Classic/Iron Age	Europe – Roman	Europe – Early Medieval	Europe – Medieval	Europe – Renaissance/Post Medieval	Europe – Early Modern	Europe – Modern	Europe – Contemporary	Europe – Multiperiod	Middle East – Prehistory	Middle East – Greek-Roman	Middle East – Islamic/Medieval/Cont.	Asia – Prehistory	Asia – Far East Civilisations	Asia – Modern/Contemporary	Africa – Prehistory/Palaeonthology	Africa – Modern/Contemporary	North America – Prehistory/Palaeonthol.	North America – Early Cultures	North America – Modern/Contemporary	Latin America – Prehistory	Latin America – Maya/Precolombian	Latin America – Pre-Inca/Inca	Latin America – Colonial/Modern	Caribbean	Oceania	Worldwide
FIYE – International Youth Exchange Foundation	X																											X
Footsteps of Man																												
Fort Garland Field School in Historical Archaeology																					X							
"Frescoes Hunting" Photo Expedition to Medieval Churches of Western Bulgaria							X			X																		
The Gabii Project	X	X	X																									
Giant Prehistoric Dolmen with Petroglyphs in Dzhubga	X																											
Gordon's Lodge Fieldschool	X	X	X	X	X	X				X																		
Great Arab Revolt Project													X															
Greek-Canadian Excavations at Argilos		X																										
Gruppi Archeologici d'Italia										X																		
Hebrew University of Jerusalem											X	X	X															
Heidelberg College Experiential Archaeological Program																					X							
Heidelberg College Summer Undergraduate Field School																					X							
The Helike Project - Archaeological Excavations	X	X																										
Heraclea Lyncestis Excavation Project		X	X																									
Historical and Social Landscapes of the Greater Yellowstone Ecosystem																			X	X	X							
Huari-Ancash Archaeological and Bioarchaeological Project																							X					
Humayma Excavation Project												X																
Huyro Project																								X				
Idalion Expedition											X	X																
Iklaina Archaeological Project	X	X																										

229

ORGANISATIONS AND PROJECTS

ANALYTICAL TABLE BY GEOGRAPHIC AREAS AND PERIODS

Organisations and Projects	Europe – Prehistory	Europe – Classic/Iron Age	Europe – Roman	Europe – Early Medieval	Europe – Medieval	Europe – Renaissance/Post Medieval	Europe – Early Modern	Europe – Modern	Europe – Contemporary	Europe – Multiperiod	Middle East – Prehistory	Middle East – Greek-Roman	Middle East – Islamic/Medieval/Cont.	Asia – Prehistory	Asia – Far East Civilisations	Asia – Modern/Contemporary	Africa – Prehistory/Palaeonthology	Africa – Modern/Contemporary	North America – Prehistory/Palaeonthol.	North America – Early Cultures	North America – Modern/Contemporary	Latin America – Prehistory	Latin America – Maya/Precolombian	Latin America – Pre-Inca/Inca	Latin America – Colonial/Modern	Caribbean	Oceania	Worldwide
Indigenous Archaeology in Australia Field School																												X
INEX Slovakia – Association for International Youth Exchange and Tourism				X	X	X																						
Ingleston Motte Research Project					X																							
International Archaeological Student Camp – Amphaxitis	X	X																										
Introductory Archaeological Geophysics Field School																											X	
Iron-Age/Celtic Necropolis of Pintia		X	X																									
Ironbridge Gorge Museum Trust								X																				
Isca Project		X	X																									
Israel Foreign Ministry											X	X	X															
Judith River Dinosaur Institute																			X									
Kabyle Archaeological Survey		X															X											
Kalat Project	X	X	X	X						X																		
Kansas Archaeology Training Program																			X	X								
Kfar HaHoresh Archaeology and Anthropology Field School											X																	
Kinneret Regional Project											X	X																
Koobi Fora Field School																	X											
Krastevich – A Greek Emporion in Ancient Thrace		X																										
Lahav Research Project, Phase IV: Tell Halif Excavations											X	X																
Lajuma Archaeological Research Project																	X											
Lamanai Archaeological Project																							X					

ORGANISATIONS AND PROJECTS

ANALYTICAL TABLE BY GEOGRAPHIC AREAS AND PERIODS

Organisation / Project	Worldwide	Oceania	Caribbean	Latin America – Colonial/Modern	Latin America – Pre-Inca/Inca	Latin America – Maya/Precolombian	Latin America – Prehistory	North America – Modern/Contemporary	North America – Early Cultures	North America – Prehistory/Palaeonthol.	Africa – Modern/Contemporary	Africa – Prehistory/Palaeonthology	Asia – Modern/Contemporary	Asia – Far East Civilisations	Asia – Prehistory	Middle East – Islamic/Medieval/Cont.	Middle East – Greek-Roman	Middle East – Prehistory	Europe – Multiperiod	Europe – Contemporary	Europe – Modern	Europe – Early Modern	Europe – Renaissance/Post Medieval	Europe – Medieval	Europe – Early Medieval	Europe – Roman	Europe – Classic/Iron Age	Europe – Prehistory
Legambiente																			X									
The Leon Levy Expedition to Ashkelon																	X	X										
Louisbourg Archaeological Program																											X	
Lubbock Lake Landmark										X																		
Magura Uroiului Archaeological Project																											X	
Maya Research Program						X																						
Middleborough Little League Site								X																				
Midwest Archeological Center, National Park Service								X	X	X																		
Montpelier Archaeological Expeditions								X	X	X																		
The National Trust																			X							X		
The Necropolis of the Roman City of Sanisera																				X	X	X	X	X		X		
Nent Valley Archaeological Research Project																				X	X	X	X					
Newbarns Project																												X
NICE – Never-ending International Work Camps Exchange													X															
North East Hants Historical & Archaeological Society																											X	
North Pennines Heritage Trust																			X		X		X	X				
Noviodunum Archaeological Project																											X	
Nuvuk Archaeology Project Excavation									X	X																		
Ometepe Petroglyph Project						X	X																					
Paleo-World Research Foundation Expeditons				X		X	X			X																		

ORGANISATIONS AND PROJECTS

ANALYTICAL TABLE BY GEOGRAPHIC AREAS AND PERIODS

Organisations and Projects	Worldwide	Oceania	Caribbean	Latin America – Colonial/Modern	Latin America – Pre-Inca/Inca	Latin America – Maya/Precolombian	Latin America – Prehistory	North America – Modern/Contemporary	North America – Early Cultures	North America – Prehistory/Palaeonthol.	Africa – Modern/Contemporary	Africa – Prehistory/Palaeonthology	Asia – Modern/Contemporary	Asia – Far East Civilisations	Asia – Prehistory	Middle East – Islamic/Medieval/Cont.	Middle East – Greek-Roman	Middle East – Prehistory	Europe – Multiperiod	Europe – Contemporary	Europe – Modern	Europe – Early Modern	Europe – Renaissance/Post Medieval	Europe – Medieval	Europe – Early Medieval	Europe – Roman	Europe – Classic/Iron Age	Europe – Prehistory
Pambamarca Archaeological Project					X																							
Passport in Time								X	X	X																		
Pella Volunteer Scheme																	X	X										
Piddington																										X	X	
Poulton Research Project																							X	X		X	X	X
Pre-Roman Culture in the Province of Zamora Project																											X	X
Projects Abroad	X																											
The Ramat Rahel Archaeological Project																X	X	X										
Rock Art Documentation and Education Project											X	X																
Roman Fort on Tyne																									X	X		
"Roman Project" Archaeological Program																									X	X		
Romans in the Mediterranean Islands: The City of Sanisera																										X		
Rushen Abbey Field School																			X					X				
La Sabranenque																					X	X	X					
Saveock Water Archaeology																												X
SCI – Service Civil International	X																		X									
Scottish Hillforts Research Program																									X		X	X
SECAR – St. Eustatius Center for Archaeological Research		X																										
Sedgeford Archaeological and Historical Research Project																									X			

ORGANISATIONS AND PROJECTS

ANALYTICAL TABLE BY GEOGRAPHIC AREAS AND PERIODS

Organisations and Projects	Worldwide	Oceania	Caribbean	Latin America – Colonial/Modern	Latin America – Pre-Inca/Inca	Latin America – Maya/Precolombian	Latin America – Prehistory	North America – Modern/Conemporary	North America – Early Cultures	North America – Prehistory/Palaeonthol.	Africa – Modern/Contemporary	Africa – Prehistory/Palaeonthology	Asia – Modern/Contemporary	Asia – Far East Civilisations	Asia – Prehistory	Middle East – Islamic/Medieval/Cont.	Middle East – Greek-Roman	Middle East – Prehistory	Europe – Multiperiod	Europe – Contemporary	Europe – Modern	Europe – Early Modern	Europe – Renaissance/Post Medieval	Europe – Medieval	Europe – Early Medieval	Europe – Roman	Europe – Classic/Iron Age	Europe – Prehistory
Semirechie and South Kazakhstan Archaeological Camp														X	X												X	
Silchester Roman Town Life Project																										X		
Sino American Field School of Archeology (SAFSA)														X	X													
Slavia Project																								X	X			
Sortino – Necropolis of Pantalica																											X	
The Speaker's House								X																				
Stara Zagora Heritage Workcamp																									X	X		
Tel Dor Archaeological Project																	X	X										
Tel Hazor Excavations Project																	X	X										
Tell es-Safi/Gath Archaeological Project																		X										
UNAREC – Union Nationale des Associations Régionales Etudes & Chantiers	X																		X			X	X		X	X		
Underwater Archaeology in the Mediterranean Sea																			X			X	X		X	X	X	
Underwater Archaeology International Field School																						X			X	X	X	
UNESCO – United Nations Educational, Scientific and Cultural Organization	X																											
Union REMPART	X																			X								
USCAP – University of Sidney Central Asian Programme														X														
Valley of Peace Archaeological Project						X																						
Villasmundo – Melilli																											X	X
Vindolanda Trust																										X		
Vive México					X																							

ORGANISATIONS AND PROJECTS

ANALYTICAL TABLE BY GEOGRAPHIC AREAS AND PERIODS

	Europe – Prehistory	Europe – Classic/Iron Age	Europe – Roman	Europe – Early Medieval	Europe – Medieval	Europe – Renaissance/Post Medieval	Europe – Early Modern	Europe – Modern	Europe – Contemporary	Europe – Multiperiod	Middle East – Prehistory	Middle East – Greek-Roman	Middle East – Islamic/Medieval/Cont.	Asia – Prehistory	Asia – Far East Civilisations	Asia – Modern/Contemporary	Africa – Prehistory/Palaeonthology	Africa – Modern/Contemporary	North America – Prehistory/Palaeonthol.	North America – Early Cultures	North America – Modern/Contemporary	Latin America – Prehistory	Latin America – Maya/Precolombian	Latin America – Pre-Inca/Inca	Latin America – Colonial/Modern	Caribbean	Oceania	Worldwide
Volunteeer Latin America																						X	X	X	X			
Volunteers for Peace International Workcamps																												X
Wadi ath-Thamad Project											X	X																
Waterway Recovery Group								X																				
Whitehall Farm			X																									
YAP – Youth Action for Peace																												X
Yavneh-Yam Archaeological Project											X	X	X															

ALPHABETICAL INDEX OF ORGANISATIONS AND PROJECTS

From the same publisher

(available from your bookstore or from website **www.greenvolunteers.com**)

Green Volunteers - The World Guide to Voluntary Work in Nature Conservation
Over 200 projects worldwide for those who want to experience active conservation work as a volunteer, also without previous experience. Projects are year round, in a variety of habitats, from one week to one year or more. From dolphins to rhinos, from whales to primates, this guide is ideal for a meaningful vacation or for finding thesis or research opportunities.
Price: £ 11.99   € 16.00 $ 16.95   Pages: 256

World Volunteers - The World Guide to Humanitarian and Development Volunteering
About 200 projects and organisations worldwide for people who want to work in international humanitarian projects but don't know how to begin. Opportunities are from 2 weeks to 2 years or longer. An ideal resource for a working holiday or a leave of absence. A guide for students, retirees, doctors or accountants, nurses or agronomists, surveyors and teachers, plumbers or builders, electricians or computer operators... For everyone who wants to get involved in helping those who suffer worldwide.
Price: £ 11.99   € 16.00 $ 16.95   Pages: 256

Archaeo-Volunteers - The World Guide to Archaeological and Heritage Volunteering
Over 180 projects and organisations in the 5 continents for those who want to spend a different working vacation helping Archaeologists. Placements are from 2 weeks to a few months. For enthusiastic amateurs, students and those wanting hands-on experience. Cultural and historical heritage maintenance and restoration and museum volunteering opportunities are also listed. The guide also tells how to find hundreds more excavations and workcamps on the Internet.
Price: £ 11.99   € 16.00 $ 16.95   Pages: 240